The Hip, the Hospital, and the Healer

40 THOUGHT-PROVOKING
REFLECTIONS FROM AN
UNEXPECTED HOSPITAL STAY

Dr. Larry G. DeLay

TRILOGY CHRISTIAN PUBLISHERS
Tustin, CA

Trilogy Christian Publishers
A Wholly Owned Subsidiary of Trinity Broadcasting Network
2442 Michelle Drive
Tustin, CA 92780

Living in the Spiritual World

Copyright © 2024 by Dr. Larry G. DeLay

Scripture quotations marked AMP are taken from the Amplified® Bible (AMP), Copyright © 2015 by The Lockman Foundation. Used by permission. www.Lockman.org.

Scripture quotations marked NASB are taken from the New American Standard Bible® (NASB), Copyright © 1960, 1962, 1963, 1968, 1971, 1972, 1973, 1975, 1977, 1995 by The Lockman Foundation. Used by permission. www.Lockman.org.

Scripture quotations marked NIV are taken from the Holy Bible, New International Version®, NIV®. Copyright © 1973, 1978, 1984, 2011 by Biblica, Inc.™ Used by permission of Zondervan. All rights reserved worldwide. www.zondervan.com. The "NIV" and "New International Version" are trademarks registered in the United States Patent and Trademark Office by Biblica, Inc.™

Scripture quotations marked NLT are taken from the Holy Bible, New Living Translation, copyright © 1996, 2004, 2015 by Tyndale House Foundation. Used by permission of Tyndale House Publishers, Inc., Carol Stream, Illinois 60188. All rights reserved.

Scripture quotations marked NKJV are taken from the New King James Version®. Copyright © 1982 by Thomas Nelson. Used by permission. All rights reserved.

All rights reserved, including the right to reproduce this book or portions thereof in any form whatsoever.

For information, address Trilogy Christian Publishing

Rights Department, 2442 Michelle Drive, Tustin, Ca 92780.

Trilogy Christian Publishing/TBN and colophon are trademarks of Trinity Broadcasting Network.

For information about special discounts for bulk purchases, please contact Trilogy Christian Publishing.

Trilogy Disclaimer: The views and content expressed in this book are those of the author and may not necessarily reflect the views and doctrine of Trilogy Christian Publishing or the Trinity Broadcasting Network.

10 9 8 7 6 5 4 3 2 1

Library of Congress Cataloging-in-Publication Data is available.

ISBN 979-8-89041-631-5

ISBN 979-8-89041-632-2 (ebook)

Acknowledgments

When I was considering just how and whom to honor and recognize regarding the writing of this book, I began to think about just what I'd experienced in this life, even within the past ten to twelve years. For instance, I have had the bittersweet occasion of having a knee replaced, gall bladder removed, an open-heart triple bypass, elbow surgery, fusion surgery on three of my spinal vertebrae, and some extensive dental work, among other things! However, in reference to the theme of this book, there was nothing that could have prepared me for the crazy time that we all went through during that year!

For instance, as you have probably guessed by the title, I had a hip replaced in 2021 that got infected, and it turned out that I was going to need to go through three surgeries before that ordeal was finally dealt with—five to six months' worth of life! Through it all, my Heavenly Father was faithful to me in every part of it! So, obviously, I praise Him first and foremost!

However, there was also one other special person whom the Lord used to both save my life a time or two and keep me alive again and again and again; one person to whom I owe my very existence every day: my precious wife, life-partner, and best friend, Cindy! I can't tell you how many times she has loved, driven, served, stayed, cleaned up after, and carried me around, just doing anything and everything that was possible to truly help me stay alive! Cindy, I honestly owe my very life to "you, the love of my life"! Blessings to you, babe! This effort is dedicated to you! You are more than worthy of any accolade that I could *ever* give to you! I love you more than life itself!

Contents

Introduction ix

Day 1 Reflection: "The Hip" 1

Day 2 Reflection: "A Prisoner with a Platform" 6

Day 3 Reflection: "The Vision of the Man at the Table" 10

Day 4 Reflection: "Where Are You?" 15

Day 5 Reflection: "Trust His Integrity" 20

Day 6 Reflection: "The Greatest Resource You Have" 25

Day 7 Reflection: "Use Your Voice to Rejoice!" 30

Day 8 Reflection: "It's Never the Wrong Time to Be
Kind!" 33

Day 9 Reflection: "Seeing Suffering Through God's
Eyes 36

Day 10 Reflection: "Divine Intersections" 41

Day 11 Reflection: "God Knows Because God Knew!" 45

Day 12 Reflection: "Prove It to Yourself!" 50

Day 13 Reflection: "How Could I Pour Into This Life
Today?" 55

Day 14 Reflection: "On the Road to Worry Mode" 60

Day 15 Reflection: "How Do You Get Along?" 65

Day 16 Reflection: "Open Doors in a Closed Room" ... 70

Day 17 Reflection: "Never Alone" 75

Day 18 Reflection: "The Most Extraordinary in the Most Unusual" 79

Day 19 Reflection: "Long Days, Short Years!" 84

Day 20 Reflection: "The Power of Scripture and Prayer" 89

Day 21 Reflection: "Listen When God Speaks" 94

Day 22 Reflection: "Seeing You the Way God Sees You".................99

Day 23 Reflection: "God's Daily Assignments" 103

Day 24 Reflection: "The Sacrifices of the Father" 107

Day 25 Reflection: "When God Says, 'No!'" 111

Day 26 Reflection: "You Drive!" 115

Day 27 Reflection: "Just Like Us!"...........................119

Day 28 Reflection: "Check the Boxes, Check the Cross!" 124

Day 29 Reflection: "When the Bottom Falls Out!" 129

Day 30 Reflection: "That Same Spirit!"...................133

Day 31 Reflection: "What Do You Want Me to Do for You?" 138

Day 32 Reflection: "Taking Him at His Word!".........143

Day 33 Reflection: "Be Still!" 147

Day 34 Reflection: "Small Things!" 151

Day 35 Reflection: "No Fear of Bad News"..............154

Day 36 Reflection: "He Was Just Like Us!"..............157

Day 37 Reflection: "Lessons from a Thorn!"............161

Day 38 Reflection: "The Good Old Days!"...............165

Day 39 Reflection: "Just the Right Word!" 169

Day 40 Reflection: "Safely Home!" 173

"In the Event of..." 177

Dr. Larry G. DeLay: Educational Background......... 180

Bibliography 183

Introduction

"You need to be in the hospital," said Dr. Brice, the physician's assistant to the orthopedic surgeon, who had just replaced my original hip about seven weeks earlier. What we also didn't know at first was what was about to happen, which led to the writing of this book and these thoughts. For you see, not only did I need to be in the hospital once again, but they were to move forward in taking out the hip that had just been installed a couple of months earlier and was now infected with something that they couldn't identify (and never did)! In fact, before it was all said and done, this little detour in my life resulted in three surgeries on the same hip that touched parts of seven months! (I know, right?)

Have you ever had an experience where something hit you on your "blind side," you didn't see it coming and had no earthly idea where it was all going to lead? If so, then thank you for joining me on this journey of revelation and insight into finding out just a little bit about what I observed in the medical field, but more importantly, what the Father had in mind in allowing this little rest-stop in my life and the life of my family, and what I learned from the spiritual realm. I, honestly, couldn't help but feel a little bit like the Apostle Paul talking about his own thorn in the flesh in 2 Corinthians 12. If you recall, Paul had this ongoing struggle; he wasn't sure where it originated, why it was there, or how he should even understand it or deal with it. When it was all said and done, Paul writes in verses 7 to 10,

> Because of the surpassing greatness of the revelations, for this reason, to keep me from exalting myself, there was given me a thorn in the flesh, a messenger of Satan to torment me—to keep me from exalting myself! Concerning this I implored the Lord three times that it might leave me. And he has said to me, "My grace is sufficient for you for power is perfected in weakness." Most gladly therefore, I would rather boast about my weaknesses, so that the power of Christ may dwell in me. Therefore, I'm well content with weaknesses, with insults, with distresses, with persecutions, with difficulties, for Christ's sake; for when I am weak, then I am strong.
> 2 Corinthians 12:7–10 (NASB)

It occurred to me early on that since this was happening, it wasn't random, helter-skelter, or out of any

THE HIP, THE HOSPITAL, AND THE HEALER

left field! The Father had strategically placed me there or had allowed it to happen, and it wasn't all about me. He puts us where He wants us to accomplish His purposes, and I realized that there was more going on than just the fact that "I have a hip infection, and we need to deal with it." One of the insights that I grabbed onto was probably best summarized by a precious little pastor's widow in our church family who texted me within the first hour that I was in the hospital for the second time.

As my friend Luann stated, "I've been in the hospital many times and had many surgeries. I went each time with this thought: *The reason I am here is not the reason I am here. It's a great place to share the love of Jesus. Go get 'em, Pastor!*"

So, in recent days, I have found myself reflecting on this little message and returning to it again and again to glean the lessons and insights that the Father has been speaking to me about and showing me during this challenging time. While our experiences may not be exactly the same, I feel that there are some common lessons that we can all learn from, glean, and apply to our lives that could be a tremendous help not only to us but to those with whom we come in contact.

In my world, I have truly felt led to summarize this experience under the title of *The Hip, The Hospital, and the Healer*. As you join me on this journey through these forty simple reflections, my prayer is that the Father will speak deeply into your heart and help you identify with where this journey has taken me and how it applies to some experiences and lessons in your own life. Thanks for coming alongside me, and if you will, please come right into hospital room number 504 with me as we seek the Lord for His insights in *The Hip, The Hospital, and the Healer*. As the Apostle Paul prayed in Ephesians 1:18–24, Paul says,

> I pray that the eyes of your heart may be enlightened, so that you will know what is the hope of His calling, what are the riches of the glory of His inheritance in the Saints, and what is the surpassing greatness of His power toward us who believe. These are in accordance with the working of the strength of His might which he brought about in Christ, when He raised Him from the dead and seated Him at his right hand in the heavenly places, far above all rule and authority, and power and dominion, and every name that is named, not only in this age but also in the one to come. And He put all things in subjection under His feet and gave Him as head over all things to the church, which is His body, the fullness of Him who fills all in all.
>
> Ephesians 1:18–24 (NASB)

Please open the eyes of our hearts, Lord!

I'll join you shortly in the first little reflection! Thanks for sharing your time with me!

—Larry

DAY 1 REFLECTION

"The Hip"

Focus: Issue!

Then Jacob was left alone, and a man wrestled with him until daybreak. When he saw that he had not prevailed against him, he touched the socket of his thigh, so the socket of Jacob's thigh was dislocated while he wrestled with him. Then he said, "let me go, for the dawn is breaking." But he said, I "will not let you go unless you bless me." So he said to him, "what is your name?" And he said, "Jacob." He said, "Your name shell no longer be Jacob, but Israel; for you have wrestled with God and with men and have prevailed." Then Jacob asked him and said, "Please tell me your name." But he said, "Why is it that you ask my name?" And he blessed him there. So Jacob named the place, Peniel, for *he said*, "I have seen God face to face, yet my life has been preserved." Now the sun rose upon him just as he crossed over Penuel, and he was limping on his thigh. Therefore, to this day the sons of Israel do not eat the sinew of the hip which is on the socket of the thigh, because he touched the socket of Jacob's thigh in the sinew of the hip.

Genesis 32:24–32 (NASB)

Dictionary.com defines "hip" this way, "Your hips are the flesh between your waist and upper leg, and they're also the bones that make up the complex joints there—the ones that make it possible for your legs to move so you can walk."

I've had some trouble with my hip lately. In fact, by the time you read these words, I have had at least three surgeries on the same hip. It is no short sell to say that I've had trouble with it. When he first looked at it, my surgeon said that I had no more cartilage; I was bone-on-bone attempting to walk. My hip just finally wore out to the point that I needed some assistance to keep walking. In fact, as we remember from the definition above, the hip is the "bones that make up the complex joints there—the ones that make it possible for your legs to move so you can walk." So, foundationally, the hip is the center point of virtually all movement of your entire body! Your ability to walk comes from your hip. If the hip is malfunctioning, then so is the walking. In physical terms, the hip is an indicator of movement and independence. In spiritual terms, the Christian life is often, if not always, referred to as a "walk." In fact, in Ephesians 4:1–3, the Apostle Paul reminds us,

> Therefore I, the prisoner of the Lord, implore you to walk in a manner worthy of the calling with which you have been called, with all humility and gentleness and patience, showing tolerance for one another in love, being diligent to preserve the unity of the Spirit in the bond of peace.
>
> Ephesians 4:1–3 (NASB)

Jacob had trouble with his hip! In fact, it happened because, in many ways, he had operated independently from the Lord for far too long. So, to rectify the situation and to bring him back to Himself, I believe the angel of the Lord touched him in the socket of his thigh (his hip) to remove a good deal of his independence and bring him to the place where he would place his entire "trust" in Him (i.e., walk with Him)! While I've been rehabilitating, I've come to realize, in a fresh new way, that there are times when the Father will allow certain trials, struggles, and even suffering to bring us back to the place where we'll be reminded that He has called us to "walk with Him." The Lord has also reminded me that I, too, have operated with my own set of independence, not always walking along with Him and often trying to work things out on my own instead of trusting Him to provide whatever I needed at the time. In fact, my own hip has taught me what the Lord Jesus taught us when He said in John 5:30 (NASB), "I can do nothing on My own initiative. As I hear, I judge, and My judgment is just, because I do not seek My own will, but the will of Him who sent Me." I can't operate effectively without healthy hips! I can't physically walk without my hip doing its job. I also can't "walk effectively" or operate spiritually in an effective manner without looking to, trusting in, or depending on Him! So, presently, that's my *issue*.

How about you? What is your *issue*? What kind of problem are you dealing with right now? What do you do when your spiritual hip goes out? Will you keep on trying to go it all alone? Will you try all of the other means of reinforcement and support that people often turn to, or will you meet with Him today and surrender everything that you are and that you possess to Him? When your spiritual hip goes out, don't panic! Stop and realize that, sometimes, the Lord will use certain difficulties in your life to reach out and teach you things that you might not learn any other way! However, the reality is that He can deal with all of your *issues*, regardless of what they might be!

Prayer for the Day: "Father, I get so caught up in what I'm doing each day that I don't often slow down enough to hear Your still, small voice when You speak to me, or I bypass the merely obvious workings of Your Holy Spirit in my life. Please 'open the eyes of my heart' so that I can truly see not only Your activity in my life but Your tender love and compassion at work within me! Thank You that You speak to me, even through something as seemingly insignificant as a hip! Help me not to miss Your involvement or Your direction! In Jesus's name, amen!"

DAY 2 REFLECTION

"A Prisoner with a Platform"

Focus: Obstruction or Opportunity?

Now I want you to know, brethren, that my circumstances have turned out for the greater progress of the gospel, so that my imprisonment in the *cause of* Christ has become well-known throughout the whole praetorian guard and to everyone else, and that most of the brethren trusting in the Lord because of my imprisonment have far more courage to speak the word of God without fear.

Philippians 1:12–14 (NASB)

Prisoner: "A person deprived of liberty and kept under involuntary restraint. Someone restrained, as if in a prison, a prisoner of his or her own conscience."

Have you ever been in jail or a prison? I have, but with a little bit of a caveat. With no disrespect intended to anyone, while I have done things earlier in my life

THE HIP, THE HOSPITAL, AND THE HEALER

that probably warranted some prison time, I have been totally blessed and protected to not ever have had to be on the prisoner's side. However, I have had the opportunity to visit countless people who were incarcerated for one reason or another, and I have also been blessed to see many of those same people do their time, get themselves together, and absolutely turn their lives around! I love that! One of the intangible realities of being a prisoner is that whatever you had originally planned, your independence, is gone, your right of choice is gone, and you are completely dependent upon and at the beck and call of other people. That was basically the situation in which Paul found himself as he was writing to the church in the region of Philippi. Now, on the surface, it could look hopeless, apart from the plan, the Presence, and the intervention of the Lord. As I stated earlier in the introduction, I had the statement made to me about being in the hospital, "The reason you're here is not the reason you're here!" Paul recognized this same dynamic, and while he was in prison in Rome, he wrote letters to the Ephesians, Philippians, Colossians, and Philemon. A significant part of the New Testament came out of the heart and the writings of Paul because he was imprisoned. He was bound. He was limited, and he could do very few things in his life at that juncture. That's, more-or-less, where I found myself as the surgeon had me come back into the hospital to remove the new hip hardware that he had installed just two months earlier. I was nowhere near what might be considered helpless, but there were things that I could do two weeks prior to the infection and surgery that I couldn't begin to do again at that stage.

As I pondered this reality, I couldn't help but think, *Sometimes, the Father will either bring into our lives or allow certain things that teach us lessons that we could have never known about unless we'd gone through that particular season of pain, difficulty, or suffering.* I learned this lesson early on in life as I was married for the first time when I was twenty years old. *We were married only twenty-three full days before finding out that she had leukemia, which led us to a ninety-day hospital stay before the Lord called her home.* While I *never* want to go through anything like that again, I would not take anything for the lessons that I learned, the people with whom I've had the privilege to come alongside, console, counsel, and encourage, and the spiritual lessons that I gleaned from that season of life.

In the situation regarding my hip, I was a prisoner of sorts, as much of my freedom, independence, and mobility had been removed at least for four to five months. However, I was also fortunate to realize early on in my hospital stay that, as the psalmist King David said in Psalm 31:15 (NASB), "My times are in Your hand." If, indeed, this is true, then it means that nothing that ever happens is random, helter-skelter, or spinning out of control. He is a Sovereign God and has total control over everything that will *ever* come into your life and mine, regardless of how it looks! Just like Paul, while in the condition in which I found myself at that point, I had the privilege to come alongside many, many people from within a context that I never would have had the opportunity to touch had I not had this physical setback.

So today, what about you? What season of life does the Father have you involved in at this particular time? Is what you are facing an *obstruction or an opportunity?* Do you feel like you're a prisoner of sorts regardless of what your circumstances seem to indicate? Please know that no matter what it looks like, your times are literally in His hands, and He's got you, even though your friends, your family, and your feelings may try to tell you something different otherwise. He, Himself, said, "I will never leave you, nor forsake you" (Hebrews 13:5, NASB). He truly uses a prisoner with a platform!

Prayer for the Day: "Father, please provide for my particular needs today. Please teach me to see the personal prison in which I find myself today as an opportunity rather than an obstacle. I know that You '[have] plans for me' (Jeremiah 29:11, NASB) and that 'Nothing is too hard for You' (Jeremiah 32:17, NASB). Please utilize and use my present, particular prison for Your glory! In Jesus's name, amen!"

DAY 3 REFLECTION

"The Vision of the Man at the Table"

Focus: Access and Acceptance!

"Behold, I stand at the door and knock: if anyone hears My voice and opens the door, I will come in to him and dine with him, and he with Me" (Revelation 3:20, NASB).

One long night, in the middle of the night, I saw one of the most vivid pictures I've ever seen in my life. Now, in the spirit of the description provided by the Apostle Paul in 2 Corinthians 12, I have no real idea whether I was actually awake or if I was still asleep; I am not sure. However, I remember the picture so clearly because I saw a man sitting at a little cubed-style kitchen table. There appeared to be an old-fashioned oil lamp sitting in the middle of the table, and there was also a book, which I took to be this man's own copy of the Bible, the clearly revealed Word of God. The man seemed to be in

THE HIP, THE HOSPITAL, AND THE HEALER

absolutely no hurry; it was just as if He was waiting patiently for someone to sit down and talk to Him.

I couldn't help but think back to something that I had run across the day before: a statement of the truth that the Lord God, our Father, created you and me for regular, ongoing fellowship with Him. That's when I realized just Who was sitting there, just looking for the next person to come by, sit down, and spend some time with Him. It was none other than the Lord Jesus, God's one and only Son! I immediately gathered that I was the one that He was waiting on to sit down so that we could fellowship together! I am amazed that there are so many of us who regularly sense, or even state, that there is absolutely no way that we should be considered worthy to even sit down and meet with Jesus face-to-face, much less go into a prolonged and productive time of fellowship with Him. Yet, remember Acts 4:13 (NASB), where the Scripture teaches us that, "Now as they observed the confidence of Peter and John and understood that they were uneducated and untrained men, they were amazed. And began to recognize them, as having been with Jesus."

As I observed Jesus sitting at that little table, again obviously waiting for *me* to sit down and talk to Him and fellowship with Him, I couldn't help but approach Him, initially, with a sense of shame for all the times when I had, previously, passed Him by at that appointed place and time, and gone my own way. The reality that hit me was that each time that I had done so, I was seeking to work everything out on my own in dealing with all of the sin, pain, suffering, and struggles that I was experiencing in my life and body. At that point, with the potential for impending surgery to completely remove the infected hip that I was living with, I realized in a fresh, new way that He was reaching out to me to say, "Larry, with everything that you have happening in your life right now, I'm here to provide for you to meet the challenges that you are going to run into! Slow down, sit down, rest, talk to Me, and let Me talk to you and let Me help you!" In fact, before it was all said and done, what He spoke to my heart was what He stated in the book of Matthew 11:28–30 (NASB) when He declared, "Come to Me, all who are weary and heavy-laden, and I will give you rest. Take My yoke upon you and learn from Me, for I am gentle and humble in heart, and YOU WILL FIND REST FOR YOUR SOULS. For My yoke is easy and My burden is light."

He also reminded me of the words found in 1 John 1:9 (NASB), "If we confess our sins, He is faithful and righteous to forgive us our sins and to cleanse us from all unrighteousness."

To take this thought one step further, if you are anything like me, I spend way too much time mulling and mourning over the sins, mistakes, and shame of my past instead of recognizing, accepting, and enjoying the fact that the Lord has already promised in His Word that, when Jesus died on the cross, He paid the entire penalty for my sins, each and every last one of them! So, in the process of it all, He reminded me to go back to Hebrews 10 and read just how completely He took care of every sin. In fact, Hebrews 10:10 (NASB) says, "By [His] will, we have been sanctified through the offering of the body of Jesus Christ once for all."

Then, Hebrews 10:12 (NASB) says, "But He, having offered one sacrifice for sins for all time, SAT DOWN AT THE RIGHT HAND OF GOD."

Finally, Hebrews 10:14 (NASB) says, "For by one offering He has perfected for all time those who are sanctified."

Jesus died one time, for all time, for all sin! So now, when I pass the proverbial table in the morning, I realize that He is fulfilling what Hebrews 4:14–16 tells us about "access" to Him when it declares,

> Therefore, since we have a great high priest who has passed through the heavens, Jesus the Son of God, let us hold fast our profession. For we do not have a high priest who cannot sympathize with our weaknesses, but One who has been tempted in all things as we are, yet without sin. Therefore, let us draw near with confidence to the throne

of grace, so that we may receive mercy and find grace to help us in time of need.

Hebrews 4:14–16 (NASB)

Don't miss this! The man at the table drew me near to Him, and He is waiting on you; now! Stop and let Him refresh your mind, heart, spirit, soul, *and* body! That's what He came to do: restore, refresh, renew, and re-establish that fellowship with all of us! Blessings to you today!

Prayer for the Day: "Father, it is sometimes hard for me to comprehend just how close You really are and how willing and longing to meet just with me! Please help me not to miss You, but thank You for providing opportunities throughout my day to get to check in and reconnect with You if I'll just look for them! Thank You that even though I am often faithless, You are always faithful! (2 Timothy 2:13). In Jesus's name, amen!"

DAY 4 REFLECTION

"Where Are You?"

Focus: Location, Position, Condition!

They heard the sound of the LORD God walking in the garden in the cool of the day, and the man and his wife hid themselves from the presence of the LORD God among the trees of the garden. Then the LORD God called to the man, and said to him, "Where are you?" He said, "I heard the sound of You in the garden, and I was afraid because I was naked, so I hid myself." And He said, "Who told you that you were naked? Have you eaten from the tree of which I commanded you not to eat?" The man said, "The woman whom You gave to be with me, she gave me from the tree, and I ate." Then the LORD God said to the woman, "What is this you have done?" And the woman said, "The serpent deceived me and I ate."

Genesis 3:8–13 (NASB)

When we were kids, we used to all gather at some-body's house and play in our neighborhood. Our neigh-borhood covered about five full blocks of houses, and we would all get together three or four nights a week and play together until dark. One of our favorite games was called "sheet board down," which was a modified game of "hide-and-seek"! We would use a broom or a shovel or rake, something with a handle, and we called that our "sheet board." The object of the game was to hide, then get back to the home base and knock down the "sheet board" without being caught! The last one standing, when it was all said and done, was the winner, as once the rest of the gang had been caught, they were out of the running to be the one to win. However, even if the last contestant could knock down the "sheet board," everyone else was freed from having been caught, and the whole game started all over again. It wasn't unusual to hear the person who was "it" crying out softly, "Where are you?" as they searched and searched for that one last remaining contestant!

When Adam and Eve sinned, they immediately re-alized that they had "crossed over"! They had sinned, they had transgressed the instructions and command-ments of Almighty God, and they were intent upon hid-ing from Him for an indefinite period of time as their nakedness, their failure, and their vulnerability were now exposed! In the truest spiritual sense, they "died," just as the Father had told them when He placed them in the garden and offered His warnings to them. Once again, as the Lord was walking in the garden in the cool of the day, He cried out to them, "Where are you?" even though He already knew exactly where they were! It's such a great question: "Where are you?"

Think about it with me for just a minute: "Where are you?" Where are you in your relationship with God the Father through His Son, the Lord Jesus? Has there been a time when you cried out to Him in repentance, asking for forgiveness of your sins and asking Him to apply His precious blood to cover each and every one of your sins? Has there been a time when you surrendered everything that you are and everything that you have to Him and asked Him to be both "in" your life and to be "the Lord" of your life? You see, the reality is that the reason that the Father asked Adam and Eve where they both were was not for His own "information." The Lord already knew where they both were! He was asking them for their own "revelation"! He wanted them to, symbolically, take a good look at where they were and be willing to tell Him, "Yes, we blew it! Yes, we sinned! Yes, we disobeyed! Yes, we went to the one place that You made it clear that we were *not* to go, and we ate of the one tree that You made it clear that we were *not* to eat from! Yes, we messed up everything!"

Now, I tell you that because while I was lying in a hospital bed for almost two weeks at one time, I had much time and opportunity to mull over the question, "Where are you?"! If and as you and I open up our hearts to the Father and we listen for the still, small voice of the Holy Spirit, that same Spirit begins to tenderly touch us, teach us, and tear away from us those things that are displeasing to Him! Yes, He already knows where you are today, and He is just waiting to hear you call out to Him for whatever you need and allow Him to meet that need! Romans 8:27 (NASB) says, "And He who searches the hearts knows what the mind of the Spirit is, because He intercedes for the saints according to the will of God." *He already knows!* He knows "who" you are! He knows "where" you are! He knows "how" you are! He already knows "everything" that there is to know about you! He knows your *location, position,* and *condition*! So, as His tender, sweet voice calls out to you from deep inside you, please know today that "He already knows," and He loves you, anyway! The beautiful part is that He will not leave you where you are if you just cooperate with Him! Once that's done, you will never have to be afraid, ever again, to hear Him say, "Hey, where are you?"! You'll be ready to meet Him right then! Beautiful!

Prayer for the Day: "Father, I know that I've run from You for a long time. Today, here I am! Here is where I am! Here is how I am! Here is what I am! Please take me, forgive me, cleanse me, fill me, empower me, and make me what You want me to be for Your kingdom and

Your glory! I worship You and adore You this very moment for Your mercy, Your grace, Your love reaching out to me, and Your incredible kindnesses! Jesus, thank You for making this relationship and fellowship possible! I honor and bless Your name right now! In Jesus's name, amen!"

DAY 5 REFLECTION

"Trust His Integrity"

Focus: Dependability!

"For I, the LORD, do not change; therefore you, o sons of Jacob, are not consumed" (Malachi 3:6, NASB).

"For God so loved the world, that He gave His only begotten Son, that whoever believes in Him should not perish, but have eternal life" (John 3:16, NASB).

> But Zion said, "The LORD has forsaken me, and the LORD has forgotten me." Can a woman forget her nursing child and have no compassion on the son of her womb? Even these may forget, but I will not forget you. Behold, I have inscribed you on the palms of My hands; your walls are continually before Me.
>
> Isaiah 49:14–16 (NASB)

I am fortunate to have been raised in the time and place where the Lord placed me. As a child, I had a great family, plenty of everything that I could have possibly asked for, and a church that directed me in the ways of Almighty God. I had a father and mother who taught me right from wrong, fed, clothed, totally protected me, and encouraged me to live in such a way that, hopefully, my life could somehow count for eternity. However, for some reason, as a small child, I had a difficult time believing that God the Father really loved me and wasn't out to get me! Interestingly enough, even as an adult believer who knows better, I have still found myself, at times, tending to wonder if the "other foot" is going to drop at some point and still wondering if God really is, somehow, looking after me! Honestly, some of this perception comes from my upbringing and what was, at times, a seeming overemphasis in the messages preached on the judgment and condemnation of God on those who, ultimately, reject Him. Now, it's not that that's not true because we know that His justice is real! But so is His amazing mercy, love, and grace toward those of us who receive His Word, repent of our sins, and turn to Him!

As I was lying in my hospital bed on Sunday morning, I got to catch a message from Dr. Tony Evans. As he closed his message, he began to tell about his little grandson who comes to the late service and always connects with him when the service comes to a close. He said that his little fellow would come up on the platform, right by the pulpit, stand right on the edge, and Dr. Evans would implore the little one to jump into his arms, down below on the floor. He said that, at first, he would basically respond, "No way," and would make his way back down off the platform. However, as time went by, Dr. Evans would get closer and closer to the edge of the platform, to the point that his grandson finally gave up and jumped into his arms! He said that this little drill went on over and over for several weeks before his grandson would jump without a great bit of cajoling. Finally, he stated that now, he barely had time to get prepared on the floor before his little guy jumped on him, almost unannounced! He said he asked his grandson one day why he did that. The little guy said, "Because I know you won't let me get hurt! You're going to catch me!"

As he reflected on this little picture, Dr. Evans said that the Lord spoke to him and shared with him that this is how God's people often approach Him, like He is not going to come through for them or us! He went on to say that the problem that most of us have in this kind of situation is that we don't really "trust" God's integrity, or His character, or His ability, or His promises, or His reliability to always provide, keep us safe, and never leave us nor forsake us! As I lay there and listened to him tell this little story, I couldn't help but bow my head in repentance and ask the Father to please forgive me for any and all of the times (and there have been quite a few) that I have doubted either His integrity, His character, His ability, His promises, or even His willingness to truly be there for me, no matter what may come my way! To put the cap on the bottle, He reminded me of what Paul wrote just as he was coming to the end of his ministry and right before he was beheaded. In 2 Timothy 4:18, the Apostle Paul sums it up for us as succinctly as one can when He writes, "The Lord will rescue me from every evil deed, and will bring me safely to His heavenly kingdom; to Him be glory forever and ever. Amen" (2 Timothy 4:18, NASB).

This verse pretty much sums up what He has taught me to depend on: His integrity! Here's the point: either God is lying, or He's going to do everything that He said just like He said it! If He said it, then you and I can truly trust His integrity and everything that comes with it! Today, regardless of what you are going through, trust Him; trust His integrity! Trust His *dependability!* He'll come through!

Prayer for the Day: Father, for far too long, I have doubted some aspects of Your amazing love! Today, I want to ask You to forgive me for questioning You, dodging You, and doubting You! You, truly, are the Lord of everything and the Lord of my life! Please forgive me for ever doubting how much You might love me when You proved it by sending Your only Son to the cross for me! Thank You for restoring our fellowship and for allowing me to be a part of Your kingdom and Your family! I bless Your name! In Jesus's name, amen!"

DAY 6 REFLECTION

"The Greatest Resource You Have"

Focus: Peace from His Power!

He will never be shaken; The righteous will be remembered forever. He will not fear bad news; His heart is steadfast, trusting [confidently relying on and believing in] the LORD. His heart is upheld; he will not fear while he looks with satisfaction on his adversaries.

Psalm 112:6–8 (AMP)

But I tell you the truth; it is to your advantage that I go away, for if I do not go away, the Helper will not come to you, but if I go, I will send Him to you. And He, when He comes, will convict the world concerning sin and righteousness and judgment: concerning sin, because they do not believe in Me, and concerning righteousness, because I go to the Father and you no longer see me; and concerning judgment, because the ruler of this world has been judged. I have many things to say to you, but you cannot bear them now. But when He, the Spirit of truth, comes, He will guide you into all the truth; for He will not speak on His own initiative, but whatever He hears, He will speak, and He will disclose to you what is to come. He will glorify Me, for He will take of Mine and will disclose it to you. All things that the Father has are Mine; therefore, I said that He takes of Mine and will disclose it to you.

John 16:7–15 (NASB)

There are some times in our lives when we have news delivered to us that we just don't want to hear! Such was the case in my life regarding the infection in my hip. At first, we were told that they might be able to open the area where the infection was centered, clean it out, and send me home with some strong antibiotics, which was going to be the case, regardless of what they did to rid me of the infection. During all of this early detection and diagnosis, the surgeon who had done my original hip replacement was out of town. So, for a time, we were under the care of four or five other doctors who were sincerely trying to offer us hope of any kind. However, the day came when our surgeon returned from his vacation and came in to see me. He delivered the message that *I did not* want to hear; he was going to go back in there, take out the new hip and everything else that he had just put in, clean out the wound as much as possible, put in a spacer, a temporary kind of hip frame that couldn't bear to have all of the weight come down on it for at least six weeks, put in a pick line for IV antibiotics that I would need to take during this six week period to finish killing out the infection that had invaded this area, then go back into surgery for yet a third surgery and put in a brand new hip joint! The fleshing out of all of this was going to take roughly another eight to ten weeks, most likely. During this time, I *could not* put all of my weight on the side where all of the hip work was done! *I did not want to hear that!* While it was not the same thing, it was like hearing that someone close to me had died. I *did not* want to hear that news!

However, I prayed a simple prayer and said, "Father, I need You to intervene in my life. I cannot deal with this on my own!" Almost instantly, I sensed His Presence, the Person of His Precious Holy Spirit entering and invading that hospital room and bringing to me the peace that only He can give, the kind that passes all understanding! (Philippians 4:6–7). Right before this news hit, I had been listening to some messages being preached, and each one of about three or four preachers had talked about "The Greatest Resource in My Life, The Holy Spirit"! I knew then that He had visited me and was right there amidst all of the fear, and doubt, and frustration, and the unknown. Honestly, I immediately turned the corner spiritually and knew that I couldn't do what needed to be done, but He could! He gave me *peace from His power!* He reminded me, in that very instant, "I can do all things through Him who strengthens me" (Philippians 4:13, NASB).

Now, the beautiful part about the Lord is that He, Himself, declares that He is no respecter of persons. What He will do for one, He will do for the other, if it is within His will! So today, please allow me to encourage you to call out to the Spirit of the Lord and ask Him into your situation, regardless of what it is, how helpless you feel, or how hopeless it looks! Remember the words of the Lord in Jeremiah 32:27 (NASB), "Behold, I am the LORD, the God of all flesh. Is anything too difficult for Me?"

Don't miss this! Call on the Spirit of the Lord, the greatest resource that you have! Trust Him and let Him do what you can't; give you *peace from His power!*

Prayer for the Day: "Father, I know that You see everything that is going on in our lives. There are things that happen that I certainly don't understand and that none of us asked for. However, I also realize that there are things that come into our lives that, whether You ordained or simply allowed them, You have every intention of using—that pothole, that detour, that frustration, and that setback—to teach us something about Yourself that we could have never learned any other way! Thank You that we don't have to go at it alone as You have sent Your Precious Holy Spirit to lead us, convict us, empower us, carry us, and do for us what we could never do on our own! Thank You that He is the greatest resource that we have available to us! Please help us to have the wisdom and insight to rely on Him, regardless of how great or small the task might appear! We need You! Precious Holy Spirit, come and take over our lives! In Jesus's name, amen!"

DAY 7 REFLECTION

"Use Your Voice to Rejoice!"

Focus: Choose to Rejoice!

"This is the day which the LORD has made; let us rejoice and be glad in it" (Psalm 118:24, NASB).

"Rejoice in the Lord always; again I will say, rejoice" (Philippians 4:4, NASB).

When you are in the middle of what could be considered an emotional mess, what you do with that mess that you are facing, how you choose to look at it, see it, and process it has everything to do with how you will make your way through it and come out of it! In fact, as we have previously looked at, Jesus, in John 16:33 (NASB), tells us, "These things have I spoken to you that in Me you may have peace. In the world you have tribulation, but take courage, I have overcome the world."

No doubt many of you have heard the story of the woman who woke up one morning to realize that she had only three strands of hair. So, she said, "Well, I think I'll braid my hair today." So, she braided her hair and had a wonderful day! When she got up the next day, she noticed that she had only two strands of hair on her head. So, she said, "I think I'll part my hair down the middle today." She parted her hair down the middle and had a great day! The next day, she woke up and realized that she had only one hair on her head. So, she said, "Today, I think I'll put my hair in a ponytail." So, she did and had another wonderful day! The next day, she woke up and realized that she didn't have a single hair left on her head. Her response: "Yes! Today, I don't have to do a thing with my hair!"

I share this little illustration with you because I read this while I was in the hospital, and it really encouraged and challenged me that my approach and my attitude toward even what is happening to me is truly up to me! It is my choice. I have a choice to be down, grouchy, and grumpy. Or, I have the choice to rejoice! It's basically up to me! And, you know what? It's basically up to you how you approach your life. It's a simple little principle, but it's incredibly profound! *Choose to rejoice!*

Prayer for the Day: "Father, there are times when I look at the things happening around me and think, *There's nothing happening in my life right now for me to re-*

joice about! Why should I be rejoicing about some of this stuff? Then, I remember that You are the Lord, and You are totally in charge and always will be! Thank You for your encouragement and Your continuous, non-stop blessings in our lives! We realize that 'Every good and perfect gift comes from You, the Father of lights, Who doesn't change, or even shift from where You are and Who You are!' (James 1:17, NASB). Thank You for always being the One we can depend on and count on, regardless of what else happens around us! Therefore, we make the choice to rejoice! We love You, Father! In Jesus's name, amen!"

DAY 8 REFLECTION

"It's Never the Wrong Time to Be Kind!"

Focus: Constant Kindness!

"He has told you, O man, what is good; and what does the LORD require of you, but to do justice, to love kindness, and to walk humbly with your God?" (Micah 6:8, NASB).

"Be kind to one another, tender-hearted, forgiving each other, just as God in Christ also has forgiven you" (Ephesians 4:32, NASB).

As I lay in the hospital bed day after day, I had the occasion and opportunity to visit with countless personnel from the hospital, including nurses, techs, helpers, kitchen staff, case workers, hospitalists, specialists of various kinds, surgeons, physician's assistants, and any number of other people associated with my case. As each one entered my room, I developed the habit of watching their body language and asking each one how they were doing and what kind of day they were having. Part of this motivation came from one particular conversation I had with one of the many nurses' aides who came in to help with the seemingly menial tasks that have to be done each and every day. As we visited, I found out that she was being given quite a bit of grief by one of the people overseeing her, as well as hearing about the way that some of the patients were reacting and responding to her. I had one of the workers tell me, "There are a couple of people I try to take care of who seem to want to ruin my day with the way that they act!" I realized then that what I have been told in past years is absolutely true, "Hurt people hurt people"! On one hand, people are not in the hospital for no reason. The ones that are in there are there because they are truly in need of medical attention. On the other hand, it is also a tremendous place to engage people in both conversation and ministry because "It's never the wrong time to be kind!"

People respond, no doubt, to all kinds of motivation. However, the most effective way to help people, bless people, and touch their lives in a personal way is with kindness, a kind look, a gentle spirit, and some soft-spoken words! Even when you and I feel horrible, we can truly make a difference in someone else's life by just turning our attention away from us, asking about them, checking on them, and approaching times of interaction with them with gentleness, with compassion, and with a kind of concern that draws them into the center of our care! People were drawn to Jesus because He wasn't like everyone else; He was different! He wasn't stuck on Him! He really cared about those around Him! So, once again, "It's never the wrong time to be kind!" There are people in each of our lives, each and every day, who are just waiting for someone to pay attention to them and care about them! Don't miss that! Jesus didn't! The key is *constant kindness!*

Prayer for the Day: "Father, I have no idea what kind of problems, struggles, difficulties, and pains those with whom I come in contact are going through today. I realize that we *all* have something that we contend with. Yet, far too often, I am so concentrated on myself and my own stuff that I fail to take the necessary time to look at the faces and into the eyes of those around me to see how they might be doing. Please help me to keep in mind the acrostic JOY: J-Jesus, O-Others, Y-You (me)! Help me to see them for who and how they really are, and help them to see You in me as I interact with them! Thank You for allowing me to serve You! In Jesus's name, amen!"

DAY 9 REFLECTION

"Seeing Suffering Through God's Eyes"

Focus: True Insight!

"These things I have spoken to you, so that in Me you may have peace. In the world you have tribulation but take courage; I have overcome the world" (John 16:33, NASB).

"For I consider that the sufferings of this present time are not worthy to be compared to the glory to be revealed to us" (Romans 8:18, NASB).

"Although He was a Son, He learned obedience from the things which He suffered" (Hebrews 5:8, NASB).

I don't know how you approach this in your own life, but the fact of the matter is that while we're in this world, you and I are going to suffer! It's just a given.

THE HIP, THE HOSPITAL, AND THE HEALER

Jesus told His own disciples this in John 16:33 (NASB), "In the world you have tribulation..." One night, as I was lying there in my hospital room, it occurred to me that there is not a human being alive who has not, does not, and will not suffer in this life, at least in one way or another. In fact, if you think about it, even little newborn babies begin to suffer the moment that they emerge from their mother's womb because everything with which they had been comfortable and had known is now just erratically changed as they enter this new world! The way it works is that things are going to continue to change throughout every season of our lives.

Now, you and I can deal with our suffering in a number of ways. We can deny it, we can hate it, we can seek to ignore it, we can try to block it from our very minds, or we can do what Jesus did in the Scripture and learn from it! There are at least three or four pretty clear purposes to suffering. One of the first purposes for suffering is that if we are going to be like Jesus, we are going to suffer just as He did because, again, suffering is just a part of life. Then, we also suffer, in the truest sense, for those around us or for those that we'll eventually encounter. There is no question that the Father utilizes the suffering in one life to help identify with and bring comfort to another brother or sister who is going through the same thing (2 Corinthians 1:3–7). Another purpose for suffering is for us to learn to obey from and through the suffering, just as Jesus did! In fact, He told the man who was healed at the pool of Bethesda, in John 5:14 (NASB), "Behold, you have become well; do not sin anymore so that nothing worse happens to you."

Sometimes, we bring suffering on ourselves. Sometimes, suffering is just our lot in life, which we have absolutely nothing to do with. As I stated previously, I married for the first time when I was twenty years of age; I was married twenty-three days before we found out that she had leukemia and entered the hospital, where she died ninety days later. In the process of all of this, I was sitting in the dark one night, musing on everything that was going on. The pain of the moment led me to cry out to the Father and say to Him, "Would You, please, let me look through Your eyes and see what You see?" as I realized that there was a great deal more going on in the big picture than just what was sitting on the surface. In fact, in my lifetime, there have been numerous times when He has been very kind to do so, and this was one of those times. I came to see and understand that my own personal suffering in that particular situation was going to be used and utilized in countless lives throughout the course of my lifetime, as I have been able to truly "identify" with people in their suffering of the loss of their loved ones, time and time again. It has brought instant understanding and comprehension to them that "I may not totally know everything that they are feeling at the moment, but we have enough common ground that they can sense that I care deeply about how they feel and have a pretty good idea of where they are emotionally and spiritually!"

Most likely, not all suffering will come with either a warning label or a clearly detailed description of exactly why we or they are going through that particular ordeal at the time. However, if we learn to look to see what the Father might be up to and ask Him to let us look into the plans that He has for us, we might be amazed at just how many insights surface as a result of the struggles that we are presently facing at that time. "But if any of you lacks wisdom, let him ask of God, who gives to all generously and without reproach, and it will be given to him" (James 1:5, NASB). That's pretty much all you need to know! Ask Him! He knows! Ask Him to let you see what He sees! That, my dear friend, is *true insight!*

Prayer for the Day: "Father, there are so many things going on in my world right now for which there appears to be no logical or reasonable explanation. Would You please take over every situation, struggle, hurt, and pain and help me to understand if there is, indeed, a lesson or lessons that I should be gleaning from them? I fully realize that I have the position of being fully human and extremely limited in my capacity to absorb all that You might be communicating, especially since You are an infinite being, and I'm certainly limited. I know that, in my life and throughout my day, there are going to be things that are going to happen that I am going to definitely need Your insight, interpretation, and understanding to wrap my head around what You are attempting to say and show me. However, I truly don't want to miss You. I don't want to miss out on Your involvement, Your participation, and Your wisdom. Please protect my heart and mind today, and please help me to keep an openness to You and to Your direction. I truly want to interpret suffering and difficulty through Your eyes. This is the only way that I can see to operate and function. Thank You for the way You teach and lead us! We love You! In Jesus's mighty name, amen!"

DAY 10 REFLECTION

"Divine Intersections"

Focus: Divine Appointments!

And He had to pass through Samaria. So, He came to a city of Samaria called Sychar, near the parcel of ground that Jacob gave to his son, Joseph, and Jacob's well was there. So Jesus, being wearied from His journey, was sitting there by the well. It was about the sixth hour. There came a woman of Samaria, to draw water. Jesus said to her, "Give me a drink." For his disciples had gone into the city to buy food. Therefore, the Samaritan woman said to Him, "How is it that you, being a Jew, ask me for a drink, since I am a Samaritan woman?" (For Jews have no dealings with Samaritans.) Jesus answered and said to her. "If you knew the gift of God, and who it is who says to you, Give Me a drink, you would have asked Him, and He would have given you living water."

John 4:4–10 (NASB)

I always marvel at the activity, the movement, and especially the timing of God! Not only does God bring together people, places, situations, and details, but His ability to coordinate all of these particular entities is absolutely amazing to me! Maybe I had never seen it more clearly than I saw it on my first day in the hospital this particular time: how He brought together one of the sweetest meetings that I have personally ever been a part of!

Along with pastoring my church, I have the privilege of serving as a corporate chaplain to a couple of corporations in the Tulsa area, where I'm on call to them for whatever way that I can serve the needs of the employees, spiritually! So, when I realized that I was going to be in the hospital for a period of time, I called the human resources director for each of the companies to explain to each of them what was happening in my hip and in my body. Each one was incredibly kind and told me to just be sure to get myself well! As I talked to one of them, I found out that a friend of mine who serves in their company in a very visible capacity had been in the hospital for several days, although almost no one else in the company knew anything about it. This HR director was merely asking me if I'd pray for the patient, but to just still not say anything! So, I told her that I absolutely would! Then, I asked her what hospital my friend was in. As it turned out, she was right down the hall from me, Room 522, and I was in Room 504! Same floor, same hospital! (Only God could have arranged that!) So, I told her that I'd try to go see her, which I was able to do two different times before we both were released from that hospital! I got to both visit and pray with her and her husband, which was a very special privilege for me! However, the greatest thing about it all was watching the Lord put it all together, with neither one of us having any idea that the other was even there! What an amazing deal!

In Psalm 31:15 (NASB), the psalmist says, "My times are in Your hand." I came to realize, in a fresh new way, that the Father is in absolute control. He's in charge, and He's working all of the time, just like Jesus told us that He is! Call them coincidences, lucky meetings, chance happenings, or however else you want to frame it. However, if the Word of God is true (and it is!), then there is no question that you and I are the blessed recipients each and every day of His "divine intersections, *divine appointments*," where the Father brings all of His resources together to carry out the plans that He has arranged for us! There are no coincidences! There are no surprises, at least not with God! There are no accidents! There are no uh-ohs! Proverbs 19:21 (NASB) says, "Many plans are in a man's heart, but the counsel of the LORD will stand." Watch for the "divine intersections"! They're some of the sweetest places you'll ever encounter!

Prayer for the Day: "Father, far too often, I get to believe that things are happening around me that are just helter-skelter; they're just happenstance, or just going to happen because there's nothing guiding, directing, or regulating their activity! Yet, every time that I read Your Word, I see again and again that You are a Sovereign God and that You are planning activities, directing traffic, and pulling together more details than any of us can possibly fathom! Thank You that, in my life, I am not just a random pinball bouncing off of the walls of life with no real control at all! Thank You that my life was planned (Jeremiah 29:11), along with the lives of everyone around me! Thank You that we are totally and completely under Your control and care! Thank You that we can depend on You to help us have exactly what we need to fully complete Your perfect will for our lives! Please forgive us when we go off on our own and try to do whatever we do apart from Your divine intervention, realizing that every intersection that we come to is a "divine intersection!" You planned it all! You truly are an awesome God! Thank You for allowing us to belong to You! I, honestly, wouldn't have it any other way! In Jesus's name, amen!"

DAY 11 REFLECTION

"God Knows Because God Knew!"

Focus: Omniscience!

Now a certain man was sick, Lazarus of Bethany, the village of Mary and her sister, Martha. It was the Mary who anointed the Lord with ointment, and wiped his feet with her hair, whose brother Lazarus was sick. So, the sisters sent word to Him, saying, "Lord, behold, he whom You love is sick." But when Jesus heard this, He said, "This sickness is not to end in death, but for the glory of God, so that the Son of God may be glorified by it." Now Jesus loved Martha and her sister and Lazarus. So when He heard that He was sick, He then stayed two days longer in the place where He was. Then after this, He said to the disciples, "Let us go to Judea again."

John 11:1–7 (NASB)

As I lay there in my hospital room for the first six days, waiting on the news about what was actually happening to me and awaiting the news about exactly what the infection might be that had invaded my hip, I was given a certain amount of hope for three or four days as the initial prognosis was that they might be able to open up the incision and clean out the infection, then go ahead and send me home. However, as I've shared elsewhere, when my surgeon returned from vacation, he brought to us the very word that I had hoped we would never have to deal with. He told us that they were going to have to go back into surgery and take out the new hip that they had just installed (that was now infected). Then, they were going to put in an antibiotic hip spacer for a period of time until they could kill the infected area. They also gave me IV antibiotics for at least six weeks through a pick line in my arm that ran straight to my heart. After two full months, the doctors went back in there and took out all that hardware. Then, once again, they put in a new hip! Now, for all I knew, I was just dealing with a hip, not necessarily a life-and-death situation, although it definitely could have turned out that way! However, I have since learned that it is an incredible blessing that the situation didn't turn fatal, even though I had no way to comprehend that at the time. In those times, it becomes fairly predictable to want to look heavenward and ask, "Lord, did You see

THE HIP, THE HOSPITAL, AND THE HEALER

this coming? Did you *know* that this was going to take place?"

When Lazarus became ill, I'm quite certain that his sisters had no real heads-up that he was just about to go through the pain and process of dying! So, when they saw him getting progressively worse, they sent word to Jesus immediately, believing that if Jesus was present, Jesus had the wherewithal and the power to prevent Him from dying. Yet, in the economy of God, it's a funny thing, sometimes, that we normally have one plan for what is going on, and God, often, has yet another! After hearing the disturbing news about Lazarus, such was the case on this particular day as Jesus stayed "two days longer" where He was! He was in no hurry to get back to Bethany, where Lazarus lay dying and, subsequently, did die! Jesus realized that God had another plan, another purpose, and that, ultimately, Jesus was going to be glorified by Lazarus's death!

It begs to have the question answered, again, "God, did You know? Do You know stuff like this? Do You know everything about each of us? Do You know who is going to live and when someone else is going to die?" Honestly, the answer that the Word of God gives us is, "Yes, He *does know*!" He knows everything! He is fully aware of everything that you and I are going through, even before we ever enter into it. Psalm 139:1–6 says,

For the choir director. A Psalm of David.

O LORD, You have searched me and known me. You know when I sit down and when I rise up. You understand my thought from afar. You scrutinize my path and my lying down, and are intimately acquainted with all my ways. Even before there is a word on my tongue, behold, O LORD, You know it all. You have enclosed me behind and before, and laid Your hand upon me. Such knowledge is to wonderful for me; it is too high, I cannot attain to it.

Psalm 139:1–6 (NASB)

With Lazarus, God knows because God knew! The word is *omniscience*—the fact that God knows everything at all times! With my hip and its detours, God knows because God knew! Whatever situation that you are going through today, God knows because God knew before you ever entered or encountered it! No, I have no idea why you might be being asked to go through this particular situation. However, don't despair because God knows what He's doing with it because He knew it was coming! As I, again, heard it said several years ago, "God is never caught off guard, shocked, surprised, nor has He ever had an 'uh-oh' or an 'I never saw that coming' moment!" Here's the reality: "If God brought you to it, God will bring you through it!" He's got you because He knows everything about right where you are!

Trust Him! "He knows because He knew!" He was about to raise Lazarus from the dead! There's no telling what He's about to do for you!

Prayer for the Day: "Father, I thank You that I don't serve a God Who doesn't have a clue about what is going on in my life, but One Who knows everything that has anything at all to do with me! I would not have the slightest idea about what to do in my life if I thought that You either didn't know or didn't care! However, You've proven to me over and over that You are, as the psalmist says, 'intimately acquainted with all of my ways!' (Psalm 139:3, NASB). Today, please help me to come to the place where I will trust You in Your sovereignty before anything ever happens today of any significance! Help me to understand that 'Sovereign' means that You are in total control of every detail of life, and You *will* take care of me and my family if I will just give You the opportunity and trust to do so! I love You, Father, and I worship You! Thank You for Your love and faithfulness! In Jesus's name, amen!"

DAY 12 REFLECTION

"Prove It to Yourself!"

Focus: Personal Knowledge!

And do not be conformed to this world [any longer with its superficial values and customs], but be transformed and changed [as you mature spiritually[by the renewing of our mind [focusing on godly values and ethical attitudes], so that you may *prove [for yourselves]* what the will of God is, that which is good and acceptable and perfect [in His plan and purpose for you].

Romans 12:2 (AMP, author's italics)

"Therefore to one who knows the right thing to do, and does not do it, to him it is sin" (James 4:17, NASB).

During a part of my own soul-searching, while recuperating, I was confronted with this verse and this version from Romans 12. The part that both stuck out and spoke to me was the line that says, "so that you may prove [for yourselves]." You know, it's one thing when you and I lead other people to think or believe something specific about us, whether there is even a shred of validity or truth as to what they think or believe about us or not. It's quite another when you and I look inside our own hearts, see what is there, and take an honest stock of what we find. Sometimes, we have to prove again to ourselves who and how we are! We do so by comparing our hearts to the Word of God to see how we really are and not some phony version of who we think we are!

I have really struggled recently within my own heart and makeup because I have come to the conviction that there are things about the way that I seek to present myself to both the Lord God *and* other people that, at times, are just absolute lies! There are times when, because of my own coveting and selfishness, I may long for something that I absolutely should not want or have. I have found that often, I am me-centered, petty, lustful or covetous, short-tempered, and hateful, even if I don't always show it clearly on the outside. At times, far too many to even want to acknowledge, I have settled for what is sheer disobedience and the abuse of grace, believing and misleading myself into believing that God will, of course, forgive me! Even though He actually will, I *know* that I'm either thinking, acting, or doing wrong right then!

So, as part of my own heart cleansing and the woodshedding of my life, for the first time in a really long time, I am going through my own set of soul-searching exercises to just see where I truly am with the Lord and to seek to bring myself closer to Him and to seek to bring Him closer to me! To do so, I believe that He gave me this set of questions to ask and answer for myself and to pass on to hopefully assist in your own soul-searching, soul-identifying process! Here they are! See if your heart resonates with any or all of them.

Am I saved? Do I truly know Jesus Christ as my own personal Savior?

Do I listen for, hear, know, and respond to the voice of God when He speaks?

Do I obey His commands? (John 14:15, 15:14)

Do I abstain from the appearance of evil? (1 Thessalonians 5:22)

Do I run from evil? (Amos 5:14, NLT)

Do I seek to know Him and His ways and grow in Him just a little more every day?

Do I regularly share His love, His message, and His gospel with others?

Am I living, existing, or dwelling with any known sin in my own heart or life right now?

Am I honest with myself and others?

What do I need to do to avoid, remove, or get rid of what I know to be disobedient or displeasing?

Will I do anything about, change, or remove what I am identifying, seeing, sensing, or knowing about myself right now?

> Test and evaluate yourselves to see whether you are in the faith and living your lives as [committed] believers. Examine yourselves [not me]! Or do you not recognize this about yourselves [by an ongoing experience] that Jesus Christ is in you—unless indeed you fail the test and are rejected as counterfeit?
>
> 2 Corinthians 13:5 (AMP)

The reality of all of this is, regardless of what any other human being thinks or believes about you, if you are honest with yourself and with God, then you truly have nothing to worry about because you have come to the place where you have proven to yourself, most of all, that you are living in the truth and that you truly abide there! That's the place that you want to be, and you, yourself, are the one that you need to prove it to! After all, God the Father already knows!

Prayer for the Day: "Father, for far too long and in far too many ways, at times, I tend to lead a double existence, spiritually, and realize that I have lied both to myself and to others! Today, I come clean with You, and I ask You to search me and help me to truly see just who I am and how I am. My prayer is that, when my examination is complete, I'll prove both to You and to myself that I have come completely clean and honest with You, that I'll know, beyond a shadow of a doubt, that I am right with You! I thank You that, through Christ, You are pleased with me through the blood of Jesus! I thank You for everything that You do for me each day to provide for the many needs that my family and I have! I bless Your name! Please continue to watch over me and keep me close to You! I need You every hour! In Jesus's name, amen!"

DAY 13 REFLECTION

"How Could I Pour Into This Life Today?

Focus: Influence!

"The things which you have learned and received and heard and seen in me, practice these things [in daily life], and the God [who is the source] of peace and well-being will be with you" (Philippians 4:9, AMP).

"The things [the doctrine, the precepts, the admonitions, the sum of my ministry] which you have heard me teach in the presence of many witnesses, entrust [as a treasure] to reliable and faithful men who will be able to teach others also" (2 Timothy 2:2, AMP).

It is no secret that, as believers in Jesus Christ, everywhere you and I go, we take Him with us! Now, on the one hand, that's a really *settling thought* because there is absolutely nowhere that we can go that He does not go with us! On the other hand, that is a really *sobering thought* because there is absolutely nowhere that we do go that He does not go with us! So, as you and I grow in Him, it becomes incumbent upon us to think clearly and choose carefully about where we are taking Him with all of the choices concerning where we are going to go. Now, along with this realization that He is with us comes another beautiful thought to ponder: since Jesus is with us wherever we go, there is nowhere that we will go, nor no one that we will run into, or that we encounter alone, or that we will face without Him! Since that is the case, then we can be assured that He will always have a purpose and a plan for each life that He allows us to meet!

I tell you that because it is really easy to forget that when the Lord puts us in front of someone, that person may, very well, need the words that He gives us to say or the smile that He gives us to offer them, or the spirit in our lives that He wants us to impart! We often hear of someone sharing their life with someone else using the illustration, or the metaphor, of "pouring" themselves out for another person! In fact, the Apostle Paul said it this way in 2 Timothy 4:6–10 and following,

> For I am already being poured out like a drink offering and the time of my departure has come. I

THE HIP, THE HOSPITAL, AND THE HEALER

have fought a good fight, I have finished the race, I have kept the faith; in the future there is laid up for me the crown of righteousness, which the Lord, the righteous Judge, will award to me on that day, and not only to me, but also to all who have loved His appearing.

2 Timothy 4:6–10 (NASB)

It's interesting because one simple definition of a drink offering says that it is (my words) "a libation, a mixed drink that can be made up of wine, milk, or oil, made often in biblical times and mixed with other sacrifices and required with every public offering." Now, if that's the case, then even a drink offering has the connotation of something literally "poured out" or "poured into" something else. Hence, that's why I would ask, "How could I pour into your life today? What part of my life, teachings, principles, or practices could I possibly pour into your life today that could or would help you grow in your faith?"

One afternoon, while I was in the hospital, one of the many excellent "hospital servants" came in, and we began to talk. As I visited with her, I quickly came to the conclusion that she needed some immediate TLC (tender loving care), the kind where someone sees or finds something positive in life and seeks to instantly affirm that life for that special quality! I say that because it was painfully obvious that she *was not* having a good day and needed to see some change as soon as possible! So, as I watched her work, I commented on just what an excellent job she was doing to keep everything so effectively and efficiently taken care of! As we continued to talk, she began to truly lighten up and even flashed a smile now and then! Before the conversation was over, I got to observe a complete change of face, spirit, temperament, and overall demeanor. In fact, the last thing that I asked her was, "May I pray for you?" She willingly said, "Yes!" What had, at one time, been a pretty sour day that was going nowhere fast turned around in just a little while. And that's how we ended our little encounter, with a prayer and a big smile!

Years ago, I heard a message by Dr. Robert Schuller where he said, "Find a need and meet it! Find a hurt and heal it!" That's a pretty good recipe for how to invest your day! So, as each day of your life unfolds, please consider making one of the first questions or prayer requests you ask the Lord within your heart as you encounter the various people you'll run into, "Lord, how could I pour into this life today? How could I make a difference?" Then, remember His promise in Matthew 7:7 (NASB), "Ask, and it will be given to you; seek, and you will find; knock, and the door will be opened to you." He'll show you!

Prayer for Today: "Father, when I look in the Word, in Acts 10:38 (NASB), it says, '*You know of* Jesus of Nazareth, how God anointed Him with the Holy Spirit and with power, and how He went about doing good and healing all who were oppressed by the devil, for God was with Him.' That's what I'd love for my life to consist of: having the anointing, power, and leadership from Your Holy Spirit to invest my day going about impacting lives and seeing hearts change on a regular basis. That would mean that those same hearts have come in contact with the life-changing truth that is found only in Your Son, Jesus Christ, and in Your Spirit's power! Father, please forgive me for when I don't take the time to discern what's going on in someone else's life, and I may not seek to pour into them. Please help me to be aware enough to even ask You, within myself, 'How may I pour into that life today?' I thank You that You never give up on me and that You are continually working to change me to be just like Your Son! Please continue to do that in me today! In Jesus's mighty name, amen!"

DAY 14 REFLECTION

"On the Road to Worry Mode"

Focus: Total Trust!

"Therefore, I tell you, stop being worried or anxious (perpetually uneasy, distracted) about your life as to what you will eat or what you will drink; nor about your body as to what you will wear. Is life not life more than food and the body more than clothing?" (Matthew 6:25, AMP).

Mode: "A manner of acting or doing; a method or way."

Staying in a hospital for any length of time is, actually, quite a lesson because there is this sense that, in every room, there is the potential for something really good to happen. Or, there could be something really life-altering, disturbing, or destructive just waiting to surface. In my own case, I had a hip that got infected with something that they never could identify. So, rather than worry about it, I had to trust that the doctors knew that there was a medication that they could give to me that would do its job and try to kill that infection, even without actually knowing what they were rooting out! The biggest difference between the doctors and the Lord God, besides the eternal obvious, is that there is nothing that *ever* happens to you and me that He is not thoroughly aware of and able to take care of, regardless of what might come our way.

As human beings, we often have this notion that there are things that happen to us that are random, out of control, and beyond the reach or management of anything or anyone in this world. You know what? That is absolutely *not true*! I mean, after all, just take the simple definition of the word "God." In its most basic form, "God" means "One who is in complete control of the situation." If, indeed, that is true, then there is, again, *nothing* that He doesn't rule over. That would include illnesses, accidents, crimes, unexpected inconveniences, injuries, mishaps, unwanted fears, and frustrations of any and every kind, and yes, even deaths! He sees them all. He knows them all. He understands them all. He's on top of them all. He's in charge of them all, and He's controlling them all!

Now, the reason that this is important is that to try and help God, we often go into *worry mode*. That's that place where we, somehow, think that He's either not moving fast enough, not doing enough, not trying hard enough, not intervening enough, not caring enough, or is possibly not capable of dealing with our situation because this one is, maybe, way too much for Him to jump in and take care of! In fact, we're pretty sure that we had better try and help out to make sure that *something* is getting done! So today, where do you find yourself "on the road to worry mode"? If you think about it, there are several categories in which we see ourselves on a regular basis in life where worry could actually move in and take over. In fact, there appear to be situations to worry about within the contexts of marriage, finances, relationships of various kinds, work issues, health, child-rearing struggles, educational concerns, and which bill to pay first, or even when, and any number of other countless categories.

I have had people tell me, "Well, you don't understand! I just have a gift for worrying! That's just my gift!" I want to respond, "No, that's that chain that's hanging around your neck that makes your life, at times, almost unbearable because worry never got any of us anywhere! It's kind of like a stationary bike! It'll go fast and hard, and you can ride on it for a really long time, but it rarely moves from the place where it started! It just has you tied down, bound, and stuck!" Honestly, that's what it looks like "on the road to worry mode"!

If that's where you acknowledge yourself to be today, please let me encourage you about something that's pretty simple! Here's the deal: either God means what He says, or He doesn't! Either His Word is true, or it's not! Either He will take care of you, or He won't, and He will come through for you, or He won't! If He's not going to come through, anyway, then why do you even go to Him at all? If you really don't believe that He's going to help you, then you're fooling yourself, in some ways, believing that He even might do something because it's obvious that you don't trust Him, at least not right now! However, if He really *is* going to come through for you, then all of your worrying is needless, useless, and worthless! It won't make a bit of difference or change a thing, and you may as well give yourself a break and just "trust Him"! And let me tell you something that I know from first-hand experience: He *will come through!* You can trust Him! So, the next time that you find yourself "on the road to worry mode," take a couple of deep breaths, then release whatever it is that you're hanging on to! He's already got it, anyway! Let it go! Total trust!

Prayer for Today: "Father, I find myself trying to pick up again and again all of those things that I have, in the past, sought to give over to You to take care of. The last time I checked, the Lord Jesus told me, in John 15:5 (NASB), 'Apart from Me, you can do nothing.' So, once again, I give my problems, my worries, my cares, my anxieties, my fears, and all of my doubts to You, the Author and Sustainer of all things! I know that You have told me that if I would seek You first, and Your kingdom, then everything else that I need would be added to me (Matthew 6:33). So, today, I cast all of my cares upon You, knowing and believing that You care for me! (1 Peter 5:7). Thank You for taking such amazing care of me and for always being faithful, even when I am not faithful! I am truly tired of traveling 'on the road to worry mode!' Please replace all of that baggage with Your Spirit's Presence, Your comfort, and Your peace! Thank You again for loving me! In Jesus's name, amen!"

DAY 15 REFLECTION

"How Do You Get Along?"

Focus: Grateful and Content!

I know how to get along and live humbly [in difficult times], and I also know how to enjoy abundance and live in prosperity. In any and every circumstance, I have learned the secret [of facing life], whether well-fed or going hungry, whether having an abundance or being in need. I can do all things [which He has called me to do] through Him who strengthens and empowers me [to fulfill His purpose—I am sufficient in Christ's sufficiency. I am ready to do anything and equal to anything through Him who infuses me with inner strength and confident peace.]

Philippians 4:12–13 (AMP)

In days gone by, people were known to greet each other with the question, "How are y'all doing?" And, it wasn't uncommon for the answer to be, "Oh, we're getting along." You might even hear one of them say, "Oh, we're makin' it," or "We're getting by," or "We're hanging in there," or "We're surviving...somehow!" It's an interesting study of people and their outlooks, their approaches, and their responses to life. Several times during my hospital stay, I asked a nurse or medical person, "How's it going?" I can't tell you how many times I heard one of them say, "I'm actually having a pretty tough day." Invariably, they would go on to tell me about what was going on in their home, or how truly overcrowded the hospital was, or how understaffed they were, even though they were, honestly, doing an outstanding job!

As I engaged one of them after the other, I couldn't help but think back to the words and example of the Apostle Paul in this powerful passage above in Philippians. In fact, if you remember, Paul spent some time in 2 Corinthians 11:24–33 telling us about his struggles. He says,

> Five times I received from the Jews thirty-nine lashes. Three times I was beaten with rods, once I was stoned, three times I was shipwrecked, a night and a day I have been in the deep. I have been on frequent journeys, dangers from rivers, dangers from robbers, dangers from my countrymen, dangers from Gentiles, dangers in the city,

THE HIP, THE HOSPITAL, AND THE HEALER

dangers in the wilderness, dangers on the sea, dangers from false teachers. I *have been* in labor and hardships, through many sleepless nights, in hunger and thirst, often without food, in cold and exposure. Apart from *such* external things, there is the daily pressure on me *of* concern for all the churches. Who is weak without my being weak? Who is led into sin without my intense concern? If I have to boast, I will boast of what pertains to my weakness. The God and Father of the Lord Jesus, He who is blessed forever, knows that I am not lying. In Damascus, the ethnarch under Aretas the king was guarding the city of the Damascenes in order to seize me, and I was let down in a basket through a window in the wall, and so escaped his hands.

2 Corinthians 11:24–33 (NASB)

As has often been stated, the word that comes to mind that seems to best explain everything that I am trying to say is the word "perspective." Perspective can, for our purposes, be most simply defined this way: "The view according to how you look at the events in your life." The reality is that we all have things that happen to us; life just happens! Often, it hurts because Jesus told us, "In the world, you will have tribulation" (John 16:33, NASB). The real key to dealing with all of it has to do with "how you look at it"! In one sense, if you are what is known as a "glass half-empty" person, then you are going to deal with the things that happen to you and to those around you in a fashion that looks at those things as if there is always something lacking; like, you and yours have always been cheated and are still being cheated by the unfair gods of life! However, if you happen to be known as a "glass half-full" person, then you are more than likely to look for the good, positive, encouraging, and the lessons that come attached to every event in life, realizing that we have an awesome, Sovereign God Who is indeed in charge of each and every phase and facet of our lives! If that is truly the case, then there is absolutely nothing that is ever going to happen to us that He is not, ultimately, responsible for either earmarking, approving, or deciding for. Again, if that is the case, then we also need to remember what Romans 8:18 (NASB) tells us when it says, "For I consider that the sufferings of this present time are not worthy to be compared with the glory that is to be revealed."

We also remember the words of the Apostle Paul when he writes in 1 Corinthians 2:9 (NASB), "For just as it is written, 'THINGS WHICH EYES HAS NOT SEEN AND EAR HAS NOT HEARD, AND *which* HAVE NOT ENTERED THE HEART OF MAN ALL THAT GOD HAS PREPARED FOR THOSE WHO LOVE HIM.'"

So, if I'm not mistaken, a great deal of "how you are getting along" in this life has directly to do with how you look at things. If you try to do it all by yourself, you'll fail miserably! However, if you look to Him, seek Him, call out to Him, trust Him, listen to Him, and believe that He has a plan and is, indeed, in control of it all, then you'll get along beautifully! You'll be *grateful and content!* You'll truly experience what He promises in Matthew 6:33 (NASB), "But seek first His kingdom and His righteousness and all these things will be added to you."

Prayer for Today: "Father, I have tried my best to 'get along' on my own, but, to this point, that is not working! So, I humbly come into Your Presence today and ask You to help me to 'get along' the way that You want me to. I realize that You have a plan for my life, as well as the lives of all of those around me, and Your heart and intentions are always good toward me. So, right now, I ask You to take away any of the doubts, fears, hesitations, and reluctances that I may have about submitting and surrendering myself to You, and please help me to 'get along well' in my life because I have given everything over to You and Your 'watch care' that I possibly can. I know that You paid a steep price for my soul with Your precious shed blood. Now, I'm asking You to truly be the Lord of everything that involves me so that I may completely 'get along' with Your blessing and Your favor! Please help me to be *grateful and content!* Thank You for always taking such amazing care of me! In Jesus's name, amen!"

DAY 16 REFLECTION

"Open Doors in a Closed Room"

Focus: Not Confined!

Now I want you to know, brethren, that my circumstances have turned out for the greater progress of the gospel, so that my imprisonment in *the cause of Christ* has become well-known throughout the whole praetorian guard, and to everyone else, so that most of the brethren, trusting in the Lord because of my imprisonment, have far more courage to speak the Word of God without fear.

Philippians 1:12–14 (NASB)

"I, Paul, write this greeting in my own hand. Remember my chains. Grace be with you" (Colossians 4:18, NIV).

While I touched on this earlier in the second reflection, I want to revisit one principle found here that absolutely fascinates me! One morning, while I was studying, the reality of Paul's situation hit me like a ton of bricks. It is no secret that in Roman tradition and practice, it was not uncommon to have a soldier or soldiers guarding a prisoner, at least one-on-one, and possibly as many as four. Now, while this may seem a little extreme to us, the lesson that stood out in such a stark fashion to me was the fact that "God was not, is not, and will not ever be limited to going where He needs to go, doing what He needs to do, or reaching into wherever He needs to reach to have His will done in a life!" While Paul was limited as to his own particular mobility, he had the "open door" of simply sharing the messages of the heart with those around him that the Lord gave to him each and every day! In doing so, we know, from his writings, that he was regularly converting the guards and servants who attended to him daily! In this way, the Word of the Lord was being spread throughout the entire praetorian system, and the kingdom was going forward, even though Paul most likely couldn't move at all! Actually, he predicts and, more-or-less, projects the same approach for you and me. Paul tells us, in Philippians 1:29–30 (NASB), "For to you, it has been granted for Christ's sake, not only to believe in him, but also to suffer for his sake, experiencing the same conflict which you saw in me and now hear *to be* in me."

So, how does that happen? How can God work when I can contribute virtually nothing?

Well, it happens because the Holy Spirit is not bound, in any way or by any means, within time, space, distance, or with any sort of man-made boundaries! In fact, in Ephesians 6:18–20, we find one of the cries of his heart that Paul made regarding this very subject when he says,

> With all prayer and petition, pray at all times in the Spirit, and with this in view, be on the alert with all perseverance and petition for all the saints, and pray on my behalf, that utterance may be given to me in the opening of my mouth, to make known with boldness the mystery of this gospel, for which I am an ambassador in chains, that in *proclaiming* it, I may speak boldly, as I ought to speak.
>
> Ephesians 6:18–20 (NASB)

One of the lessons that Paul demonstrates to us is that he never allowed anything; not hardships, not difficulties, not sickness, not famine, not torture, not beatings, not threats, not taunting, not hunger, and not even ongoing chains to prevent him from sharing what the Lord had placed on his heart. Nor did it prevent him from sharing with whomever God placed in his path! In this way, Paul always had "open doors in a closed room"! The key: as long as the Holy Spirit is present, there is truly no limit as to what can happen, and there is no barrier that can prevent the Word of God from going forward to whomever it needs to go, regardless of how it may look at the time! It totally fascinates me how Paul operated all the time, allowing nothing to keep him from completing the call that God had placed on his life to take His Word wherever God led him. Paul was *not confined*! In fact, we see this in his final letter and final reflection, just shortly before he died. He writes in 2 Timothy 4:6–8,

> For I am already being poured out as a drink offering and the time of my departure has come. I have fought the good fight, I have finished the course, I have kept the faith; in the future, there is laid up for me the crown of righteousness, which the Lord, the righteous judge, will award to me on that day, and not only to me, but also to all who have loved his appearing.
>
> 2 Timothy 4:6–8 (NASB)

So today, don't forget God always has "open doors in a closed room," regardless of how it looks! He is never bound, limited, or prevented from accomplishing that which concerns you, me, and His perfect will! He is *not confined*! As the psalmist says, "The LORD will accomplish what concerns me" (Psalm 138:8, NASB). There you go!

Prayer for the Day: "Father, I absolutely marvel at how You can live and move and get done whatever is on Your plan and Your plate for me and for each and every one of us each day! I fully realize that we have no idea just how amazing You really are and how magnificent and powerful are Your works and Your ways! Today, I thank You that You never gave up and You never give up on me, regardless of how human, willful, and sinful I have shown myself to be to You! You are amazing in all Your ways! Today, please allow me to see, once again, something of Yourself that I have never seen before regarding how You can open the door when I can, at times, barely move a muscle! I realize that this is how You operate all the time, and often, I just don't see it! Today, please let me see You and Your outpouring! I love You, and I truly desire to serve You, regardless of what else comes at me! Help me to glorify You today in all that I do! In Jesus's mighty name, amen!"

DAY 17 REFLECTION

"Never Alone"

Focus: Constant Companionship!

Behold, an hour is coming, and has already come, for you to be scattered, each to his *own home*, and to leave Me alone, and yet I am not alone, because the Father is with Me. These things I have spoken to you, so that in Me you *may* have peace. In the world you have tribulation but take courage. I have overcome the world.

John 16:32–33 (NASB)

Where can I go from Your Spirit? Or, where can I flee from Your Presence? If I ascend to heaven, You are there: If I make my bed in Sheol, behold, You are there. If I take the wings of the dawn: If I dwell in the remotest part of the sea, even there Your hand will lead me, and Your right hand will lay hold of me. If I say, 'Surely the darkness will overwhelm me, and the light around me will be night, even the darkness is not dark to You, and the night is as bright as the day. Darkness and light are alike to You.

Psalm 139:7–12 (NASB)

There are times in our lives when we are left to feel that we are completely alone; everyone else has left, and we're all by ourselves in the battle in which we find ourselves. I guess if I'm completely honest, there were a couple of nights in the hospital when I let pity and "woe is me" sort of take over, and I would have to catch myself and remind myself that I was not alone in that hospital room, even though everybody else had gone home. In the words of Jesus, "The Father is with me." As I was lying there, I began thinking about some of the places that I've been blessed to travel to in this world, some of the destinations. A number of years ago, I had the privilege to go to Nigeria on a trip that lasted about twenty-three days. I was actually in three different small villages over nine days in the middle of absolutely nowhere! As I reflected on that experience, the Lord reminded me of the feeling and the sentiment I had that very first night when I looked up at the stars and said, "Well, Father, it's just You and me. If You're not here, then I'm in real trouble!" I had the same conversation with Him several years later on a trip to India, where we stayed again for around twenty-two or twenty-three days. While I was around people all of the time, I felt totally alone at times because there was nothing familiar to me that was around me. However, once again, He reminded me that He was there with me, and I had absolutely nothing to fear!

When my boys were little and just learning to walk, they would try to strike out on their own. Each one of them wanted to be independent in trying to handle their own mobility all by themselves. We would come to a set of steps, and each time, they would want to try to navigate those steps all by themselves. So, to try to give them as much independence as possible, I would stick out my little finger and encourage them to take hold of it. To them, the initial appearance was that they were totally in control. What they didn't understand was that I had three other fingers and a thumb ready to grab them in a heartbeat once I saw them beginning to struggle or possibly fall. It was during those times that the Father would speak clearly to my own heart, and He would say to me, "I do you exactly the same way! Much too often in life, you want to try to navigate the steps of life, the ups and downs, the hills and the valleys, all by yourself, and I have never intended for you to live that way. I want you to trust in Me and look to Me and depend on Me to carry you over those tough spots!" Then, He would remind me, "Don't forget; you are *never alone*! I am right here with you, regardless of where you go or what you run into!"

Today, please allow me to encourage you that you are in the same situation right now! Regardless of how it looks, how it appears, how it feels, or what it seems like, you are not alone whether you are in your home, in your car, at your job, or in a secluded place where no one else is around; God is right there with you! You are *never alone*, and you never will be! In Hebrews 13:5 (NASB), He reminds us, "I WILL NOT DESERT YOU, NOR WILL I EVER FORSAKE YOU."

Let Him carry you today and help you! He's right there! Just say His name and see what happens!

Prayer for the Day: "Father, I am really hurting today because, 'yes, I truly feel all alone today!'" I search Your Word, and I see what it says, and I'm encouraged by the words of the Lord Jesus when He declared that He, also, wasn't alone because You were with Him! Today, please bring comfort to my hurting heart and heal me from these haunting thoughts that the enemy keeps bringing to my mind! Please shut him down and overcome my own doubts and fears. I am looking to connect with You in a fresh, new way today! Thank You for Your continuing Presence and for the fact that You are truly with me regardless of how it looks! I know that I am *never alone* because You are here! I love You, and I wait patiently to hear from You. You are all that really matters! I worship You, Lord! In Jesus's mighty name, amen!"

DAY 18 REFLECTION

"The Most Extraordinary in the Most Unusual"

Focus: God's Innovation!

"And the LORD appointed a great fish to swallow Jonah, and Jonah was in the stomach of the great fish three days and three nights" (Jonah 1:17, NASB).

"Then the LORD commanded the fish and it vomited up Jonah onto the dry land" (Jonah 2:10, NASB).

All throughout the Word of God, we have examples of how God worked in amazing, extraordinary ways in what would be considered some of the most unusual places! For instance, God told Noah to build a structure called an ark, and God had him build it with very specific instructions that included the dimensions, the materials, the arrangement, and the exact details of everything that God wanted done. God had Noah do this because God's plan was to restore the world that He had created, and He was using Noah to do it whether Noah fully realized it or not. In Egypt, God used a set of plagues to demonstrate His power to both His own people and to the Egyptians. He used both the parting of the Red Sea and the Jordan River so that His people could cross over to the other side each time and so that they would know that there was nothing that was too hard for Him! He used a burning bush as a speaker system to tell Moses that he was to deliver God's people from Egyptian bondage! He used a talking donkey to rebuke a disobedient messenger. He used the deliverance of three men in a fiery furnace, heated seven times hotter than normal, to demonstrate His power to deliver them by demonstrating their untouched safety and His total control. He used the spoken Word over the outside elements to calm a storm and to calm the hearts of His disciples who were afraid that they were about to die in the deep water! He used a man named Philip to share His gospel message with an Ethiopian eunuch, riding in a chariot in the middle of nowhere so that the gospel could be taken to the Eunuch's part of the world. He protected David in a fight with a giant and also protected him in a cave from another man trying to kill him. He sheltered Daniel in a lion's den and delivered a woman from death by stoning who had been taken in adultery.

THE HIP, THE HOSPITAL, AND THE HEALER

In the passage above from the book of Jonah, God had instructed Jonah to go to the city of Nineveh and to preach a message of warning to them that they needed to repent. However, Jonah tried desperately, using all his own might, to get away from the call of God and to run as fast and as far as he could because he didn't want to go to Nineveh. Jonah learned a very valuable lesson through this little experience. Sometimes, God will send a detour into our lives to remind us that He is God, to accomplish His will, and to help fulfill the plan that He has put in place. That's what God did with Jonah! Jonah had gotten into a boat to continue to try to get away from the Lord. However, God orchestrated the events of the evening in such a way that Jonah ended up in the deep water, being swallowed into the stomach of a very large fish! Here, he lived for the next three days and three nights as God protected him, instructed him, corrected him, directed him, and then safely brought him back to dry land! The reality of it all is that God can do anything and everything, utilizing anything and everything, to accomplish His purposes!

I say all of this because while I was going through the process of watching a very serious infection be removed from my body over a period of two months and watching my body be healed (that was, in its own way, definitely "life-threatening"), I, too, was blessed to see God do some amazing things and work in some amazing ways! I had the opportunity to pray with and pray for many people; I've had the privilege of seeing people come to know Christ as Lord and Savior during this process. I have seen God change the hearts, lives, and destinies of several people, and I watched Him do it in hospital rooms, doctors' offices, three or four funeral services, and even in my own home! As these things unfolded, I realized our Heavenly Father is not bound by time, space, or distance in any way, shape, form, or fashion! He is God, and He does the extraordinary in the most unusual places and ways! Don't let today go by without watching for the activity of Almighty God all around you! He is the *God of Innovation*! You will be amazed at what He does!

Prayer for the Day: "Father, I never cease to be amazed at how You operate. Your Word tells me that Your mercies are new every morning, and every day is a brand-new day with You, one that is full of new events, situations, and surprises! So, when I see the way that You so graciously moved in Jonah's life and I recall just how kind You have been in the way that You have moved in my life, I come to realize afresh and anew the fact that You do some of Your most amazing work in places that the average person would never think to look unless they happened to truly be purposely looking for You! Today, as we make our way through the traffic patterns of our lives, please "open the eyes of our hearts" to see what

You may be doing right in front of us that we would have missed had we not been looking for Your unique activity! You are moving in so many different ways each and every day that float right past us because we haven't been prompted or trained to look for You! Please help us to *not* miss what You are up to! You might even have it in Your plan to include one of us in Your amazing activities today! Thank You! In Jesus's mighty name, amen!"

DAY 19 REFLECTION

"Long Days, Short Years!"

Focus: Fickle Time!

"So teach *us* to number our days so that we may present *to you* a heart of wisdom" (Psalm 90:12, NASB).

"So then, be careful how you walk, not as unwise men, but as wise, making he most of your time, because the days are evil" (Ephesians 5:15–16, NASB).

I have never understood this whole thing about time. From the time I was a small child, I have been baffled by the fact that when you wait on something, it seems to take forever. For instance, when I was younger, I couldn't wait until I got older, and I thought it was never going to get there. I remember being in activities like football practice and band practice and meetings and thinking, *Is this ever going to be over?* The days seemed so long, and in many ways, they were. However, as time passed, I came to realize that each hour is exactly the same length, and it carries the same amount of opportunity, possibility, creativity, or waste! It all depends on what you do with it.

As I was lying there in the hospital, I couldn't help but think back on my thoughts from the past and think about a number of the different things that I have been through in life. I remembered the day that I came to know the Lord Jesus Christ as my personal Savior, and what a great day that was! I thought back to the day that I was baptized. I recalled the experience that I had with the Lord when I was a teenager at Falls Creek, our summer youth church encampment. That special night, I got my pastor and father in the ministry, Robert Griffin, out of bed to tell him that I believed that the Father was calling me to serve somehow in ministry! I think back to the hours and hours that I invested in teaching myself to play the guitar, bass guitar, and other musical instruments (and I genuinely loved every minute of it)! I can still clearly remember the countless classes that I invested in seminary training and seeking to become the "best" pastor that I possibly could be! I think of all of the places that the Lord has allowed me to go for the privilege and opportunity to serve Him and the people I have had the blessing to meet as a result of doing so!

I also couldn't help but think through some of the many, many times of sin and failure that I have been a part of in my life: the rebelliousness, the direct disobediences, the sometimes seemingly heinous nature of some of my actions, the no doubt criminal context of a few of those things! I realized that if anything good or worthwhile has ever come from me, it is because of His grace, mercy, unending kindnesses, and love that I am fully aware of that I never have and don't deserve from Him! Yet, I'm still here, so there must be a plan still in place for me to seek to live out and fulfill.

As I was reflecting on the confusion that "time" sometimes brings to us, I couldn't help but remember the old adage found in today's reflection title that stated, "The days are long, but the years are short." I don't know if I've ever been aware of what turns out to be a more strategic and clear-cut statement than that one. Sometimes, we wonder if the particular day that we're experiencing is *ever* going to get over with, and then the next thing that you know, we're into the next day and the next! Solomon sheds some pretty clearly defined insight in Ecclesiastes 3:1 (NASB) when he states, "There is an appointed time for everything. And there is a time for every matter under heaven."

However, the number one lesson that I think the Father has taught me is, "While days, at times, truly do seem really long in their daily carriage of events, life really is short!" Remember with me today that, in God's economy, every second of every minute matters, and there is nothing that is wasted, misplaced, or that doesn't count! Time may appear quite fickle to you and me at times. However, remember what James writes in James 4:13–14,

> Come now, you who say, "Today or tomorrow we will go to such and such a city and spend a year there and engage in business and make a profit." Yet you do not know what your life will be like tomorrow. You are just a vapor that appears for a little while and then vanishes away.
>
> James 4:13–14 (NASB)

We often hear it said, "It'll be gone before you know it!" I'm beginning to realize that truth more and more every day! So, allow the Father to help you to "count your days" because the time is truly short! Don't allow *fickle time* to throw you off! Beginning right now, make the most of every day count for the kingdom of God! You'll be eternally grateful that you did so!

Prayer for the Day: "Father, the gift of time is the greatest gift that You have ever given to us, second only to the gift of life itself! We praise You today that You have allowed us the privilege to live, breathe, and know You in a personal, intimate, life-changing, life-altering way through Your Son, the Lord Jesus Christ! Thank You that Your Word tells us that You have a plan and a purpose for each and every one of us. Help us to truly discover that purpose and to live it out to the fullest of what You want to accomplish in and through us in bringing Your kingdom to full fruition! Also, thank You that You have chosen us to be a part of helping to fulfill those kingdom purposes! Today, please teach us to look accurately at this day that we have before us here on this earth and help us to make the most of each one thereafter! We love You! In Jesus's precious name, amen!"

DAY 20 REFLECTION

"The Power of Scripture and Prayer"

Focus: Double-Edged Provision!

"All Scripture is inspired by God and profitable for teaching, for reproof, for correction, for training in righteousness, so that the man of God may be adequate, equipped for every good work" (2 Timothy 3:16–17, NASB).

"Then, beginning with Moses and with the prophets, He explained to them the things concerning Himself in all the Scriptures" (Luke 24:27, NASB).

"[B]ut sanctify Christ as Lord in your hearts, always being ready to make a defense to everyone who asks you to give an account for the hope that is in you" (1 Peter 3:15, NASB).

Often, I am genuinely approached by people with really solid, sincere questions about all sorts of life subjects, ranging from marriage questions to questions about the Bible or theology or the End Times, or difficult subjects like divorce and remarriage, or suicide, or even how the Lord God views certain things. While this wasn't a question, the principle was the same. I was on a mission trip to India a number of years ago, and I had a pastor hand me his newborn baby and say to me, "You name him!" So, I responded, "You want *me* to name your newborn son?" He replied that, "Yes," he did! So, you know what I do when something like this happens? I turn to the only two sources of leadership and direction that I know of that are absolutely reliable and trustworthy: prayer (which I did *right then* with the baby boy) and Scripture (which ultimately answered my question in this situation). (*Hint*: I'll give you the name at the end of today's reflection, which came directly from Scripture.) In James 4:2 (NASB), James tells us, "You do not have because you do not ask."

So, that definitely affirms the place of earnest prayer. Therefore, each time a new situation arises, I continue to learn to seek the leadership of the Lord "on the spot," so to speak, trusting Him that He's going to come through immediately if I just ask and trust.

Then, there's the other resource: Scripture! I have discovered that there is real power and authority in

Scripture because it truly is the written, inspired, without error, without failure "Word of God!" In fact, remember the declaration from the writer of Hebrews 4:12 (NASB), where he states, "For the Word of God is living and active, sharper than any two-edged sword, even penetrating as far as the division of soul and spirit, of both joints and marrow, and able to judge the thoughts and meditations of the heart."

So, the real question to answer is, "How do you view both the Bible and prayer? Are they just other religious symbols and practices, something to check off that you have attempted to engage in, or for you, are they what is often referred to as "life and breath"? The story is told that evangelist Gipsy Smith was talking to a man who said that he had received no inspiration from the Bible, although he had gone through it "several times." So, Smith remarked to him that he needed to "Let the Bible go through you once, then you will tell a different story." I joyfully and totally concur with that conclusion! The more of the Bible that I get inside of me, the more I get rid of myself and the rest of the world that I have allowed into my life! That's why John 15:3 (NIV) says, "You are already clean because of the word I have spoken to you."

In Ephesians 5:25–26 (NIV), Paul writes concerning both wives and the church, "Husbands, love your wives, just as Christ loved the church, and gave himself up for her, to make her holy, cleansing her by the washing with water through the word."

That's why Hebrews 4:12 (NIV) says, "For the word of God is alive and active. Sharper than any two-edged sword, it penetrates even to dividing soul and spirit, joints and marrow; it judges the thoughts and attitudes of the heart."

Today, read the Word of God to see what He has to say to your heart. Allow the Father's *double-edged provision* to work its way deep into your soul and life! Then, ask Him for what you need, remembering, "Now to him who is able to do immeasurably more than all we ask or imagine, according to his power that is at work within us, to him be the glory in the church, and in Christ Jesus throughout all generations, forever and ever! Amen" (Ephesians 3:20–21, NIV).

By the way, the baby boy's name is "Solomon"! As I prayed, I asked the Lord to give this little guy wisdom! When I prayed for that to happen, the Holy Spirit brought the name "Solomon" to mind since we glean a great deal of insight from the wisdom and writings of Solomon! I know, right? Again, "Double-edged provision: Scripture and prayer!"

Prayer for the Day: "Father, we are so grateful today to be able to call You Father and to know that there is nothing that will ever come to our lives that You are not ultimately in charge of and responsible for. We thank

You that in Your divine wisdom, You make provision in ways that we can't comprehend and with a power that we can't understand! Thank You that You're the Lord of everything and that You give us the double-edged provision of Scripture and prayer to lead us, guide us, connect us, and sustain us. We have no idea where we would be without You, and we never want to find that out! Thank You again for everything! We love You! In Jesus's name, amen!"

DAY 21 REFLECTION

"Listen When God Speaks"

Focus: The Promptings!

"Trust in the LORD with all your heart and do not lean on your own understanding. In all your ways acknowledge Him, and He will make your paths straight" (Proverbs 3:5–6, NASB).

> My sheep hear My voice, and I know them, and they follow Me; and I give eternal life to them, and they will never perish; and no one will snatch the, out of My hand. My Father, who has given them to Me, is greater than all, and no one is able to snatch them out of the Father's hand. I and the Father are one.
>
> John 10:27–30 (NASB)

"Whether you turn to the right or to the left, your ears will hear a voice behind you saying, 'This is the way: walk in it'" (Isaiah 30:21, NIV).

THE HIP, THE HOSPITAL, AND THE HEALER

"And God said, 'Let there be light,' and there was light" (Genesis 1:3, NIV).

"The Spirit Himself bears witness with our spirit that we are children of God" (Romans 8:16, NASB).

I recently overheard a well-known, highly respected Bible teacher say that someone asked him if God actually has a voice and speaks to us. His answer was something like, "In all honesty, I would have to say, 'No, He doesn't have an actual voice. We don't actually hear His voice.'" Now, I don't want to pick a fight with anyone. However, in its original form and application, the Hebrew word *dabar* both denotes and connotes "communication, transmitting a message," however you want to say it. In fact, one of the basic definitions of the word "voice" is "to give utterance or expression to; to declare, proclaim." Again, the basic idea is simple communication! Now, does God actually "speak"? If He does, how does He do it? I'm not totally sure, other than to take at face value the verse that I quoted at the beginning of this little reflection, where Genesis 1:3 (NIV, author's italics) says, "And God *said*, 'Let there be light.'"

Or I couldn't get past the simple message found in Romans 8:16 (NASB), where the Apostle Paul writes, "The Spirit Himself bears witness [He *communicates*] with our spirit that we are children of God."

In his book *Experiencing God*, Dr. Henry Blackaby says that "God speaks to us by the Holy Spirit through the Bible, prayer, circumstances, and the church to reveal Himself, His purposes, and His ways." That means that He uses virtually each and every thing that He has created to make us aware of His Presence and influence, regardless of where we go or what we might be experiencing at that particular time in our lives.

I don't know. I don't want to make too much out of this, but I think that it is, actually, a fairly important issue. "Does God have a voice?" I have no real idea! However, since His Word says, "And God said," then I have to assume that "yes," He does, indeed, have a voice and does, indeed, *speak*! I would say this to you, though. Rather than getting all caught up in the semantics, I think it is probably more accurate to express that "God has a clearly understood method of communication" when He is ready to get a message to us! In fact, back to Isaiah 30:21 (NIV), the verse tells us, "Your ears will hear a voice behind you."

The Hebrew word for ears is the word *ozen*, which is defined as the organ of hearing. So, regardless of how technical that one wants to get, the fact of the matter is that there is no question that the Father "communicates," He *prompts*; He "transmits a message" to the "ears of the heart," or the spirit of man, when He wants a man or woman to hear what He is saying to us.

During my hospital stay, I had countless *promptings* from the Lord over any number of things, not the least

THE HIP, THE HOSPITAL, AND THE HEALER

of which was the inner speaking and leading from His Spirit to ask someone who had come into my room, "How are you doing today?" Often, that one simple question led to that person both unpacking and unloading what was on their heart at the time, which led to having the opportunity to pray for them right there on the spot. People sometimes look at me with a questioning expression that says, "Do you really do that right then?" My response to them is, "Yes! Right then is when they need prayer and encouragement the most!" And that comes when we are listening closely to the speaking *(prompting)* of the Lord into our hearts, minds, spirits, and lives!

Today, you and I are going to encounter many, many different situations and experiences that we are not, by nature, going to know how to handle. However, He has promised in James 1:5 (NASB) that, "If any of you lacks wisdom, let him ask of God, who gives to all men generously and without reproach, and it will be given to him."

My friend Curtis has a son who is an air traffic controller in Los Angeles, California, at LAX, one of the busiest airports in the world. In fact, Google says that they have an average of around 1,650 flights per day! So, if you are a pilot, you are totally dependent on the information that the air traffic controller provides for you, telling you where to go, when to turn, how to approach, and what to do with every move! He is watching the entire screen, seeing all that is going on. It only makes sense to rely on his insight, perspective, and direction!

In the same way, since the Word of God tells us that our Heavenly Father is "omniscient" (all-knowing), it only makes sense that we would ask Him what He would have us do since He can see the entire screen of life from His vantage point. Yes, it only makes sense that we should "ask God," listen when He speaks, and follow His *promptings*! It's truly the only way to fly!

Prayer for the Day: "Father, there are so many things about You that will probably continue to remain a complete mystery to me. One of them is exactly how You speak. There's no question in my mind that, however we define it, You have the greatest capacity in the world to communicate Your message to us. The obvious key to the whole thing is for us to listen, observe, watch, and respond. Please forgive us when we are stubborn, guarded, and skeptical, not simply acknowledging the things that are obviously right in front of us: Your world, Your creation, and the events that You orchestrate to speak to us on a daily basis! Thank You that You love us enough to draw us to Yourself! Help us not to miss that! Please lead us today! We love You! We need You! In Jesus's precious name, amen!"

DAY 22 REFLECTION

"Seeing You the Way God Sees You"

Focus: Invaluable!

But you are a chosen people, a royal priesthood, a holy nation, God's special possession, that you may declare the praises of Him who called you out of darkness into His wonderful light. Once you were not a people, but now you are the people of God; once you had not received mercy, but now you have received mercy.

1 Peter 2:9–10 (NIV)

"For He made Him who knew no sin *to be* sin for us, that we might become the righteousness of God in Him" (2 Corinthians 5:21, NKJV).

When you look in the mirror, what do you see? Each morning, I have the privilege to see my beautiful wife get prepared for the day as she goes through her routine of carefully applying the beginning and finishing touches to hair, makeup, clothing, shoes, and overall appearance, and I always marvel because she has a definite outcome in mind every time she begins the process, and *always* hits the mark! By way of contrast, when I look in the mirror in the morning, I often tell people, "Well...we just work with what we have!"

While there is absolutely no doubt in my heart and mind that I am, indeed, a sinner saved by His unfathomable grace, somewhere along the way, I was led to believe that I was a "worthless, basically good-for-nothing failure, *nobody* who couldn't and wouldn't get it right, no matter how hard I tried!" I'm not totally sure where all of that came from, but there is a huge part of that thought process that has seasoned a good portion of my life for a very long time! However, recently, the Lord has initiated several things in my existence to allow me to see things differently; in fact, to truly look into and see things the way that His Word says that He sees them!

I have been reminded of something that I mentioned earlier that I need to elaborate on. When I was married for that brief period earlier in life (before she passed away from leukemia), there was a night in my own heart and walk with the Lord where, as I lay there in bed, I looked up toward heaven and said to the Father, "Please, let me look through Your eyes and see what You see," because I realized there was more going on than just what was sitting on the surface before me! Beginning that night, and even up to this day, He has been extremely kind to do so, to allow me to see many things the way that He sees them. So, lately, one of the things that He has been clearing up, retooling, and reinforcing to me is that "I am *not* a worthless, basically good-for-nothing failure, *nobody* who can't and won't get it right!" No, I am a child of God who is, obviously, so treasured in the eyes of the Heavenly Father that He sent His one and only Son to die on a cruel cross for my sins and my soul so that I could be what the Bible calls "redeemed," bought back, paid for, and recreated! My heart, soul, spirit, and life are *invaluable!* So are *yours!* He proved it to you and me when He died on a cruel cross for us! In fact, in 1 Peter 1:18–19 (NASB), Peter tells us, "[K]nowing that you were not redeemed with perishable things like silver or gold from your futile way of life received from your forefathers, but with precious blood, as of a lamb unblemished and spotless, *the blood* of Christ" (NASB).

You and I are "the righteousness of God in Christ" (2 Corinthians 5:21). That's what His Word teaches us! While there is so much of this that I will probably never comprehend, we are *invaluable* in the eyes of Almighty God, or the Lord Jesus would have never paid the price that He did so that we could have a relationship with the Godhead! What an incredible, unthinkable, incomprehensible, absolutely "indescribable gift"! (2 Corinthians

9:5). What a truly unexpected outcome! That's the way the Father sees us—*invaluable!*

Prayer for the Day: "Father, I don't even know where to begin to know how to process what You've done for me! The gift of Your Son, His sacrifice, my sins being removed, and my salvation being given to me is so much more than my finite mind can ever fully comprehend! Lord, I just want to once again say thank You for giving me the blessed privilege to belong to You, to know You, to communicate with You, to fellowship with You, to cry out to You, to receive from You whatever I need in this life because You told me You would take care of me and my family! I love You so much! I worship You! Thank You again! In Jesus's precious name, amen!"

DAY 23 REFLECTION

"God's Daily Assignments"

Focus: Flexible Service!

"The mind of man plans his way, but the LORD directs his steps" (Proverbs 16:9, NASB).

> And they passed through the Phrygian and Galatian region, having been forbidden by the Holy Spirit to speak the word in Asia; and when they had come to Mysia, they were trying to go into Bithynia and the Spirit of Jesus did not permit them, and passing by Mysia, they came down to Troas. A vision appeared to Paul in the night: a certain man of Macedonia was standing and appealing to him, and saying, "Come over to Macedonia and help us. And when he had seen the vision, immediately we sought to go into Macedonia, concluding that God had called us to preach the gospel to them."
>
> Acts 16:6–10 (NASB)

While completing these reflections, I bought a new journal. This journal is a unique approach to daytime planning because it offers a number of very practical daily applications. For instance, there is a place for a daily fitness goal. There is a place for a daily general goal. There is a box that says, "Today I feel inspired by..." There is a section that evaluates what is a good and bad food day. There is a place to record that, for which I am grateful today. There is a page for daily activities, actions, and goals. Then, there is a summary page that seeks to evaluate what kind of day I have had overall. In all reality, it is a well-organized piece of work that should serve me quite well if I use it regularly.

I share all of this because, as I was preparing to write these words today, I couldn't help but think through what I believe that the Lord showed me about yesterday and how both yesterday and today apply to "every day." The reality is that every day, I awaken and set out to try to lay out or plan the things that I believe I can see that need to be done, accomplished, and taken care of. Then, invariably, an event will take place, a phone call will come, something will happen, and the entire day will be turned upside down from what I had originally intended or believed to be what was going to occur.

Such was the case for yesterday! Yesterday, I was asked to come to a breakfast meeting with some friends who are planning a trip to Africa later in the summer.

Then, following breakfast, I was on my way to take care of some weekly responsibilities that were mine to cover. However, before we could leave breakfast, I received a text from a lady who is a member of my church, telling me that her mother had been in an accident and had been taken to a hospital and was likely to have some surgery. Then, just after I left, I drove only about six or seven miles before receiving a phone call from one of my deacons checking to see if I happened to be going by a certain hospital and asking if I might be able to run by to see a neighbor friend of theirs, which I did and was glad to do. While this is only a small sampling of what happened "yesterday," it is a fairly accurate description of what happens "every day," as the Scripture tells us that we plan what we *think* are the things that need to be done each day, but the Lord, more-or-less, directs and redirects our steps. That's why Psalm 23:3b (NASB) says, "He guides me in the path of righteousness for His name's sake."

Psalm 138:8a (NASB) says, "The LORD will accomplish that which concerns me."

Not only does God get His will done, but He also takes care of what He is truly trying to do by often involving you and me and accomplishing what is best for us. For us to be in on what He is doing, we need to have an attitude and approach of *flexible service*, that of being willing to follow "God's daily assignments" whenever they show up! I don't know what you have planned to try to get done today, but the Lord will not only allow divine interruptions but bring in and bring on those very same interruptions to get done His kingdom work! Often, it'll come right through you and me! Reality: *flexible service* is what He's after.

Prayer for the Day: "'Open the eyes of my heart, Lord, so that I can see You!' Each day, I realize that Your mercies are new. I also realize that I need Your daily direction; actually, I need Your direction and leadership minute by minute to tell me what to do, show me how to do it, and give me the grace, strength, and tools that I need to actually get it done! You, alone, are the Lord, and I trust You to provide for each and every single step of the way because, without You and Your direction, I have no idea where I'm going. Thank You that You allow me to serve You! As I prayed earlier, 'Open the eyes of my heart, Lord, so that I can see You!' I worship and honor You right now, today! In Jesus's name, amen!"

DAY 24 REFLECTION

"The Sacrifices of the Father"

Focus: Sacrificial Love

"See how great a love the Father has bestowed on us, that we would be called children of God; and such we are" (1 John 3:1, NASB).

"Greater love has no one than this, that one lay down his life for his friends" (John 15:13, NASB).

"For God so loved the world, that He gave His only son, so that everyone who believes in Him will not perish, but have eternal life" (John 3:16, NASB).

I don't know that I really understood or could comprehend the love of a father until I actually became one. Intuitively, I have known my whole life that my Heavenly Father really loves me. Yet, He confirmed it to me as I was growing up by sending me the very best dad

He did to raise me, to take care of me, to educate me, to prepare me, and then to send me out into the world to do the things that the Lord had prepared for me to do. He did an "incredible" job being my dad! I couldn't have had a better one for me, personally!

As I was lying there in the room one day, I couldn't help but remember two or three instances where my dad demonstrated amazing sacrifice to show me that he loved me and how much like my Heavenly Father he was in those very specific moments. For instance, in my senior year in high school, we played Dad's hometown team in football, and we were fortunate enough to beat them that night. Being a kicker, I actually had the privilege to score a couple of times, so I was grateful to be a part of the victory. When the game was over, I looked on the field, and there stood my dad right next to me. As I looked at him rather quizzically, he informed me that he had grown up with the people in that town, and he knew how "life and death" some of them were about their football and unhappy that they'd be about losing the game. So, he had come out on the field to be sure that I was safe after the game. Another time, I really needed a new electric guitar and amplifier, but we really didn't have a lot of extra money. However, my day took me to the music store and basically emptied his savings account, purchasing for me the professional-grade equipment that I wanted to get and honestly

THE HIP, THE HOSPITAL, AND THE HEALER

needed. Another time, after Cindy and I had married, we lived in Salina, KS, and I needed to have my wisdom teeth taken out. To do so, because each of them was deeply impacted, I ended up spending two nights in the hospital for the procedure to have them surgically removed. On the morning of the surgery, at about 6:30 a.m., I looked up, and there stood my dad at the door of my hospital room. Because I was going under anesthesia, he wanted to be there with us, and he had driven all night long to get there (six hours!) just to be sure that I was going to be okay! Such incredible love! Such an incredible investment! Such an incredible sacrifice!

Many times as a parent, as a dad, I have either stopped what I was doing, rescheduled what I had planned, or given up something personal to me, whether it was finances, personal rights, or especially time, so that I could be with my kids, provide for my kids, encourage my kids, support my kids, or give to my kids whatever they happened to need at the time. You know what? I don't have "one regret" about any of that, and I would do it all again! It is the greatest joy in the world to be able to invest in my own children and now in my grandchildren, whatever it is that they need!

The kicker to all of this is that God the Father literally "gave up" His only Son so that you and I could know Him personally and so that we could have a permanent home with Him in heaven that Jesus is, even now, preparing for you and me! It is the greatest example of *sacrificial love* that can be found anywhere! While this little account is rather trite and quite worn out, and probably everyone has heard it:

The story is often told that the Lord Jesus was approached by someone one day and asked, "Jesus, how much do You love me?" In the greatest illustration of love ever witnessed, He stretched out His arms to each side as far as they would reach, hung on a cross, and said, "This much!" Then, He died!

Don't *ever* question the *sacrificial love* of the Father for you and me! He has already gone to *the greatest lengths* to prove that love! His love is unquestionable, unfathomable, and incomparable! What *great* love the Father has bestowed upon us!

Prayer for the Day: "Father, I don't stop often enough to remember, recall, or reevaluate just how absolutely incredible Your love really is! However, today, I want to give praise and honor to Your name, the place where praise and honor are due! You, alone, are Lord and worthy of all the glory and honor that can be given to and bestowed upon any worthy recipient! I worship You today, Lord, and I bless Your holy name for giving me the privilege to call You my Father, to be called Your son, and to have the opportunity to wait on the place and the home that You promise that You are preparing for me! I love You, and I praise Your holy name! In Jesus's precious name, amen!"

DAY 25 REFLECTION

"When God Says, 'No!'"

Focus-Trusting Acceptance!

"They passed through the Phrygian and Galatian region, having been forbidden by the Holy Spirit to speak the word in Asia: and after they came to Mysia, they were trying to go into Bithynia and the Spirit of Jesus did not permit them" (Acts 16:6–7, NASB).

There are times in our lives when we would like certain things to be done in a certain way to suit our own likes, tastes, and interests when the Lord will have what is done to be done His way instead of ours. After my first hip surgery caused an infection, and I had to go back into the hospital for treatment and two more surgeries, there was about a five-day period when we were being encouraged to believe that there was a great possibility that the doctors would not have to go back in there to do surgery again but that they might be able to open up the original incision, thoroughly clean out the new hip joint, give me some antibiotics and close it up, again, without having to completely replace everything. However, the day came when the surgeon's PA (physician's assistant) came in to let us know that the surgeon would be back in town the following morning, and he'd probably tell us that he'd have to go back in and take out the entire original hip replacement and go from there, which is exactly what happened!

Now, I didn't want to hear that at all! I wanted them to do exactly what they had been telling us that they would probably do: open it up, clean it out, doctor it, and close it up again, waiting for it to heal. However, in the providence and will of God, that is not what they did. As it turned out, the decision that the doctors made was absolutely the right one and probably saved my life in the long run. That infection that I had, as I have previously stated, was never identified as to its origin or makeup. However, they were eventually able to completely kill that infection and totally do away with it. They absolutely made the right decision for me and my well-being!

In our Scripture today, the Apostle Paul and his team are seeking the leadership of the Lord for where He would have them go for their next assignment. As we saw it, they endeavored to go in one direction, but the Spirit forbade them. Then, they thought that they

THE HIP, THE HOSPITAL, AND THE HEALER

would go another way. Once again, the Spirit of God said, "No!" So, why does God say "no"? As I see it from both the Word of God and from personal experience, there may be two or three reasons, all of which are legitimate and may be applicable according to the need of the hour.

For one thing, when He says "no," He is, sometimes, protecting or delivering us from someone or something that we may not be able to see right now but is for our protection, personal benefit, or well-being. At other times, He says no because it simply is not His will for us to take that direction or make that choice in our lives and for His kingdom. At yet other times, God says "no" because He has us right where He wants us, regardless of how it may look at the time. There are certain lessons that you and I learn by Him saying "no" and us staying put right where He has us that we could never learn any other way! We come to know a completely different side of Him by doing so.

I have absolutely no idea why the Father might be saying "no" to you today. However, I do know that when you and I come to know Him in the personal way that He desires, then we will also know that there is nothing that is going to come into our lives that compromises His love or best interest in our lives and He will always act in our behalf and with His eternal kingdom's design in mind! The best thing that we can do is to respond with *trusting acceptance*! That acceptance is one sure sign that we truly do love Him, trust Him, and depend on the fact that He would never decide anything but what is best for us! Remember: when God says "no," respond to Him with *trusting acceptance*! That's the right way to handle it! He's got you! Trust Him!

Prayer for the Day: "Father, there have been so many times when You have told me 'no,' and I know that I didn't understand at the time. However, I have also learned that when You tell me no, there is a greater purpose that You are working out, or You are somehow protecting me from either myself or something else. I thank You that when I can't begin to see what You are looking at or seeing coming before me, You are already there and are directing me in the exact path that You want me to go! Thank You for being my God and for always covering me, regardless of whether I can see it or not. I love You! In Jesus's name, amen!"

DAY 26 REFLECTION

"You Drive!"

Focus: Relinquishing Control!

"The mind of a man plans his way, but the Lord directs his steps" (Proverbs 16:9, NASB).

"Father, if you are willing, remove this cup from Me; yet, not My will, but Yours be done" (Luke 22:42, NASB).

The story is told that one evening, on his way home from work, a man stopped off at one of the local drinking establishments to relax a little before finally continuing on to his homeplace. After imbibing in several rounds, he was then ready to proceed when a friend asked him for a ride, not realizing just how much liquor the gentleman had consumed. After driving for a few minutes and narrowly missing several head-on encounters, the passenger friend then suggested that maybe the gentleman should allow someone else to finish getting both of them home, as it seemed that he wasn't quite clicking on all cylinders with his response times. However, the man would hear nothing of the sort and politely responded, "You don't need to worry! God is my co-pilot!" Whereupon, the passenger responded, "Then, why don't you let Him drive before you kill all of us!"

There are times in our lives, if not nearly always, when we want to try to "control" every detail of life that comes our way, not realizing that we actually have very little control over anything as it is right now! In many ways, that truth is never more apparent than when one finds oneself in a hospital bed with little or no movement, as there is little or no "say" in what happens next in that life! Such was the case for me, over and over! It is one thing to be able to, as the Scripture says in Acts 17:28 (NIV), "Live and move and have our being." Even that verse teaches us that all of that happens "in Him"! "In Him we live and move and have our being" (Acts 17:28, NIV). It is quite another thing to have that "freedom of movement" somehow suddenly taken away and be at the mercy of both medical personnel and even your own physical limitations because something has happened to you that has taken away that freedom from you. Yet, keep in mind that Jesus taught us in John 15:5 (NASB), "I am the vine, you are the branches; he who abides in Me and I in him, he bears much fruit, for apart from Me you can do nothing."

It's interesting how the Lord Jesus makes a great point for us as He prays His own "gut-wrenching" prayer in the Garden of Gethsemane when He realizes that His time is near to go to the cross and the weight of the burden of our sin, the responsibility of the task, and the physical torture that He is about to endure is, at that moment, overwhelming to Him as the "Son of Man." But it is as if Jesus looked to the Father, and in words that we would understand today, He said to Him, "You drive! We'll go the way that You want us to go!" Even then, He was teaching us by example! Jesus was *relinquishing control*! That's what He asks us to do: *relinquish control*!

Let Him have His way with You! As I have stated often and will state again, "He's got this, and He's got you!" He promises that He will never leave you nor forsake you (Hebrews 13:5). So, today, tell Him, "God, You drive so that we can all arrive at home safely! I know that You are taking care of everything! I trust You!"

Prayer for the Day: "Father, for far too long, I have tried to take care of, handle, manipulate, control, and manage each and every detail of my own life. But, I continue to realize that my way is not working. It has not worked in the past. It certainly doesn't seem to be working at the present time, and I sincerely believe that it is not going to work as I go forward into the future. So, today, I am *relinquishing control* of all of it! I hand You the keys to my life and ask You to drive and take me to wherever You want me to go and do with me whatever You want to do. I realize that I don't know the way home, but You do! So, I give myself to You! Thank You for taking such amazing care of me! I love You! In Jesus's name, amen!"

DAY 27 REFLECTION

"Just Like Us!"

Focus: Identifies!

"Therefore, in all things He had to be made like His brothers so that He might become a merciful and faithful high priest in things pertaining to God" (Hebrews 2:17, NASB).

> Therefore, since we have a great high priest who has passed through the heavens, Jesus the Son of God, let's hold firmly to our confession. For we do not have a high priest who cannot sympathize with our weaknesses, but One who has been tempted in all things just as we are, *yet* without sin. Therefore, let's approach the throne of grace with confidence, so that we may receive mercy and find grace for help at the time of our need.
>
> Hebrews 4:14–16 (NASB)

In life, when you are experiencing something difficult or life-altering, it is one thing to have someone tell you, "Yeah, I know what you mean" or, "Yeah, I know exactly what you are going through," when they have never experienced anything really close to what you are experiencing right then. It is quite another when they say to you, "I don't know exactly how you feel, but I have a pretty good idea of what you're dealing with right now, and here's why!" Then, to have them proceed to tell you their story, and you come to find out that they really have walked through something fairly close to what you are walking through at that given moment, can be one of the most encouraging aspects of life that any of us can grasp because we find out that we're not alone in our journey.

In considering the prospect of having even one hip surgery, I have subsequently encountered countless people who have also had the same thing happen to them. As the infection set in after the first surgery and two other surgeries ensued, I also ran into and spoke with many, many people who had to blaze the same trail that I was on in having multiple surgeries; sometimes, three (such as I had), or four, or five, or six! Sometimes, that person's hip would be replaced, only to get infected again and again, so that when I began hearing other's stories, I eventually found myself being grateful for the fact that I had only the three surgeries to deal with over time. Yet, I also realized that these same folks had not only a grasp of what I was going through, but they really did *identify* with the pain, process, suffering, and steps it took to get through to the other side of the whole ordeal!

Now, while He was, is, and will always be Almighty God, the Lord Jesus came to this earth so that He could truly live "just like us," exist "just like us," operate "just like us," be "just like us," and *identify* with everything that you and I will ever go through! That's why Hebrews 4:15 (NASB) reminds us, "For we do not have a high priest who cannot sympathize with our weaknesses, but One who has been tempted in all things just as we are, yet without sin."

Imagine that one of these days in heaven, you and I will have the opportunity and privilege to talk "face to face" with the Lord Jesus, and we'll have the occasion to discuss with Him each and every one of the difficulties that we have encountered during our stay on this earth. Just imagine having the privilege of hearing Him speak out clearly and directly to us, "Yeah, I know exactly what you mean," and realizing that He really does get it because He walked through exactly what it is that we walked through, or it was close enough that He certainly didn't miss the point! He *identified* by becoming a human being "just like us" and walking through exactly what you and I are going through right now! That's why we can see Him as He was made "just like us" so that He could *identify* with every single detail of our existence!

That's also why Philippians 2:5–11 encourages and exhorts us,

> Have this attitude in yourselves which was also in Christ Jesus, who although He existed in the form of God, did not regard equality with God a thing to be grasped, but emptied Himself, taking the form of a bond-servant, and being found in the likeness of men. Being found in appearance as a man, He humbled Himself by becoming obedient to the point of death, even death on a cross. For this reason, also, God highly exalted Him, and bestowed on Him the name which is above every name, so that at the name of Jesus, EVERY KNEE WILL BOW, of those who are in heaven and on earth and under the earth, and that every tongue will confess that Jesus Christ is Lord, to the glory of God the Father.
>
> Philippians 2:5–11 (NASB)

However, please also be reminded of the truth found in Romans 8:18 (NASB), which tells us, "For I consider that the sufferings of this present time are not worthy to be compared with the glory that is to be revealed to us."

Today, recognize the fact that you and I are not alone because the Father sent His Son to be "just like us" so that He could absolutely *identify* with each and every situation that we will encounter! Just as He *identifies* with us, may we also today follow and fulfill the sentiment of Philippians 3:10–11 (NASB), where the Apostle Paul encourages us, "That I may know Him, and power of His resurrection and the fellowship of His sufferings, being conformed to His death, in order that I may attain to the resurrection of the dead."

Yeah, that's our ultimate goal!

Prayer for the Day: "Father, I thank You that as I walk through this difficulty, this struggle, this battle in which I find myself today, I am never alone because You have promised that You are with me and You will never leave me, nor forsake me! (Hebrews 13:5). Thank You that the Lord Jesus suffered, bled, died, and endured more difficulty and struggle than any of us will ever comprehend so that we can have the confidence and assurance that what we are going through is only temporary and we'll get through it with Your mercy, grace, and help! Help us to always remember that Your grace is sufficient and that Your strength is made perfect in weakness (2 Corinthians 12:9). Thank You for always providing, even when we can't see it or don't understand at the time! Thank You that You were "just like us"! We love You! In Jesus's name, amen!"

DAY 28 REFLECTION

"Check the Boxes, Check the Cross!"

Focus: Evidence!

For this reason the Father loves Me, because I lay down My life so that I may take it again. No one has taken it away from Me, but I lay it down of My own initiative. I have authority to lay it down, and I have authority to take it up again. This commandment I have received from My Father.

John 10:17–18 (NASB).

"For God so loved the world, that He gave His only begotten Son, that whoever believes in Him shall not perish, but have eternal life" (John 3:16, NASB).

"But God demonstrates His own love toward us, in that while we were yet sinners, Christ died for us" (Romans 5:8, NASB).

THE HIP, THE HOSPITAL, AND THE HEALER

There are times in our lives when things happen to us, and we can't help but wonder directly, "What did I do to cause this situation?" Or, "Is there something that I could've done or not done to have kept this thing from happening?" When we are diagnosed with or encounter something that is obviously going to significantly alter our lives or the lives of those around us for an extended period of time, it causes any and all of us to question any number of things, including "God, do You still love me? Have I done something to trigger this whole episode? Am I the reason that I or we are going through this difficult time? What did I do to bring this on? Am I the cause of all of this?" Probably just like you, there were times I couldn't help but lie there at night and ponder just how I got into that situation and if there was anything that I could've done to have prevented it, and yes, ask, "God, are You and I okay?"

Now, I don't claim to have the intelligence, the skills, or the acumen of a good attorney. However, I have always been fascinated by the observational skills of the people in that profession as they attempt to sort out the facts and pertinent information found in every case that they seek to try and oversee. One of the statements that we often hear is, "Check the boxes. Where does the evidence lead?" Now, in doing so in a situation like this, there are several discernible areas that we can look into to see where they lead us and what they teach us. For instance, the first one is in the area of the sheer existence of God Himself! "Is He real? Is He really here? Does He care? How much does He care? Is He trustworthy? Can I truly give over the control of my life to Him to depend on Him to take care of me, regardless?" As I seek out the evidence, there is no question that He really is here and is with me, as I have seen over and over throughout my life His heart and His hand tenderly leading and guiding me through all of the deep trials and struggles that I have encountered, yet still live to tell about it! People can try to dispel or refute His sheer existence. However, I know Him personally, and there's nothing like an eyewitness in a courtroom to authenticate the validity of a subject matter. *Check that box!*

Then, I consider what He says, His Word! Is it reliable? Is He reliable? It, honestly, becomes quite simple; either He truly is here, or He isn't. Then, either He means what He says or He doesn't, and either He will do what He says or He won't! Not too complicated. Now, having seen Him confirm and honor His Word throughout the course of my lifetime, I am convinced that His character is solid because His Word is solid and never changes! He *is* Who He says He is, and He *does* what He says He will do! That also includes every one of His promises! He honors His Word and brings to pass all that He says that He will do all throughout His Word! *Check that box!*

Next, I consider practical illustrations of this love that He claims to have for me. "Has He, somehow, demonstrated or proved that love in a practical, tangible way? Is there something to which I can point and say, 'Yeah, that pretty much nails it down and proves it?'" That's when I *check the* cross! When I look at the cross, I can't help but remember Jesus's words that are found in John 15:13 (NASB), where He states, "Greater love has no one than this, that one lay down his life for his friends."

So, when I stop and think about whether God, through His Son Jesus Christ, really loves me, I need only to *check the cross* and the fact that Jesus Himself stated clearly,

"No one has taken it [my life] from Me, but I lay it down of My own initiative" (John 10:18, NASB).

He has demonstrated quite clearly that He loves you and me and has provided the ultimate example and illustration of that love by willingly offering Himself on that cross! Without a doubt, there is more than enough *evidence* that He truly does love us and will take care of any and everything that has anything to do with our lives and well-being! What a tremendous comfort to sense Him saying, even in the most difficult times, "We're good! I've got you! I'm going to take care of you!"

When you're not sure, *check the boxes, check the* cross! Look for the *evidence!* It's all around you!

Prayer for the Day: "Father, there are times when we're tempted to look at the circumstances all around us, and they seem to scream that everything is all out of whack and have no rhyme, reason, or purpose. For instance, when there is a bad accident or an apparently untimely death, those things cause us to pause and even cause us, at times, to question what is happening, why it is happening, or even if You still love us. But then, when I go back and check the overall evidence, I realize that as I *check the cross*, I can more easily *check the boxes* because the *evidence* is so obvious, clear, and overwhelming! Thank You that You have made Your love so clearly seen and understood! I love You, Lord! In Jesus's name, amen!"

DAY 29 REFLECTION

"When the Bottom Falls Out!"

Focus: Your Problems or His Promises?

"For He Himself has said, 'I will never desert you, nor will I ever abandon you" (Hebrews 13:5c, NASB).

> And we know that God causes all things to work together for good to those who love God, to those who are called according to *His* purpose. For those whom He foreknew, He also predestined to become conformed to the image of His Son, so that He would be the firstborn among many brothers *and sisters.*
>
> Romans 8:28–29 (NASB)

"'For I know the plans that I have for you,' declares the LORD, 'plans for prosperity and not for disaster, to give you a future and a hope'" (Jeremiah 29:11, NASB).

"God is our refuge and strength, a very ready help in trouble. Therefore, we will not fear, though the earth shakes and the mountains slip into the heart of the sea" (Psalm 46:1–2, NASB).

Every time that I think about the picture of the mountains slipping into the heart of the sea, I recall several years ago when parts of the coast of California began basically having extreme episodes where great sections of the sides of the mountains would, literally, landslide into the Pacific Ocean. I remember one particular news account of a group of people who were living on the third story of their apartment complex, overlooking the edge of the ocean. The foundation upon which their facility was built had begun to severely erode, falling away little by little, to the point that about one more bout with the danger of landslide threatened to take down the entire structure! However, when interviewed, these same people had decided that they were not going to move but would take their chances with whatever came. If the house went down, they'd just go down with it! I remember thinking at the time, *I'm not sure that's the best way to go about this: to approach living in a place that could, likely, come completely down and show itself to be the location of, potentially, impending doom!*

When you and I receive news that we never wanted to hear, it can easily be likened to the mountains slipping into the heart of the sea. It could be an unwanted

THE HIP, THE HOSPITAL, AND THE HEALER

medical diagnosis, the failure of a business endeavor, the loss of income, a job, a relationship, or even a loved one! Whatever that communication happens to be, that news can be painful, life-changing, devastating, or even earth-shattering! The reality is that whatever you and I do with that news has everything to do with what kind of internal, spiritual foundation has been carefully constructed within each of us! It also has everything to do with where we happen to put our focus at the time. Will we focus on the *problems or the promises?*

When the Lord Jesus died on the cross, the disciples must have, no doubt, felt helpless, empty, and, yes, even devastated as their beloved Master had died! They watched Him die, so they realized that He was gone, but they were still there, and they were still trying to figure out how to process everything that they'd just witnessed! Their proverbial "mountain" had just fallen into the heart of the sea! So, realizing that that was real life that they never saw coming, what did they do with that? What do you and I do with that when the bottom falls out? First, we need to remember the promises:

"I will never desert you, nor will I ever abandon you."

"We know that God causes all things to work together for good to those who love God, to those who are called according to His purpose."

"I know the plans that I have for you, plans for prosperity and not for disaster, to give you a future and a hope."

"God is our refuge and strength, a very ready help in trouble. Therefore, we will not fear though the earth shakes and the mountains slip into the heart of the sea."

Then, we need to realize that everything that happens is truly part of a much greater plan, and nothing is simply random! "I know the plans that I have for you." Finally, we mustn't forget to focus on the power of the One Who is behind all of it and is taking care of us! He promises to do so, and He also promises, "I will never leave you nor forsake you!" He's got us! He's got you!

So today and every day moving forward, where will you place your focus: *your problems or His promises?*

Prayer for the Day: "Father, right now, today is an especially hard time because I'm still processing everything that is happening to me at this given moment. However, I also realize that the way that I handle all of this has everything to do with how I look at it and where I focus my attention and my trust. Today, I choose to trust You and the precious promises that You have given me all throughout Your Word! I thank You for the assurance that You will never leave me and for all of the ways that I have already seen You provide for me during my walk with You! Please help me today to stay fixed and focused on those promises and to trust in each one of them so that I can stay connected to You! I want You! I need You! I trust You! I love You! Thank You for being right here with me! In Jesus's name, amen!"

DAY 30 REFLECTION

"That Same Spirit!"

Focus: Resurrection Power Within!

"[W]hich He brought about in Christ when He raised Him from the dead and seated Him at His right hand in the heavenly places" (Ephesians 1:20, NASB).

"But if the Spirit of him who raised Jesus from the dead dwells in you, He who raised Christ Jesus from the dead will also give life to your mortal bodies through His Spirit who dwells in you" (Romans 8:11, NASB).

There are times in this life when the problems, struggles, difficulties, obstacles, and challenges look absolutely insurmountable to you, and you wonder, "How in the world am I going to deal with this thing?" If you think about it, the reality of life is that it is made up of, virtually, one challenge after another, and the sheer process of life calls upon you and me to learn to navigate those challenges, regardless of what, how, or when they painstakingly, daily, regularly present themselves to us, again and again (and again)! At some point, there will likely come for you that same moment that came for me, what the Greek language calls a *Kairos* moment; that "moment in time," that "critical crossroad" where you realize that your own resources are not, cannot, and will not be enough to carry you through whatever particular difficulty has surfaced at the time! So, when that happens, what do you do?

Please allow me to encourage you to do what I finally did! I can't tell you exactly how or when I arrived at this "crossroad," but it changed my life forever in the most positive way! I, somehow, realized that stuff kept coming day after day that I didn't ask for, I didn't expect, and I never saw coming when it did come in. There would be struggles and interruptions that I really didn't want to mess with, but there they were, ready to be confronted if and when I thought that I had the strength to do so. However, I also finally realized that I seemingly never had that inner strength that I needed on my own, but He apparently did! When I began to absorb the truth that the same Spirit that raised Jesus from the dead lives in me, I finally realized that I didn't, and I don't, have to be the source of whatever help and assistance that I need at the time because His life and resurrection have already provided whatever provision that is required for me. The reality is that He has promised that since He made me, He knew and He knows what is best

THE HIP, THE HOSPITAL, AND THE HEALER

for me; He will provide for me, He will cover me, and He will take extremely good care of me if I just trust Him!

So, at that critical juncture, I finally said, "Father, I read what You are saying to me, that I have been given that same Spirit and power that raised Your Son from the dead. There is no way that I can wrap my head and my heart around that truth. However, I believe what You are telling me! Since that is the case, I now understand that the bottom line is that You are going to take care of me or You are not! Since You have promised that You are, I surrender myself to You, and I ask You to move in and take care of this situation over which I have absolutely no control! This is Yours! I am Yours! Please deliver me; heal me; provide for me and my family; help me to do that which I have no way to do for myself! I can't do this alone, but Your Word tells me that 'I can do all things through Christ' with His strength and the Spirit of His *resurrection power within* me! Thank You that I don't ever have to try to do anything in my life like this again on my own because You are here, living within me! From now on, I depend totally on You and Your power and provision! Thank You for always being so faithful to both Your Word and to my need!"

Now, I wouldn't be so naïve or misleading to tell you that all of the problems and struggles have suddenly just disappeared, as that is simply not true! However, I will tell you that by coming to that critical juncture in my life and just simply unloading my "wagon of worries" to Him, He did, indeed, take over and has proven to be absolutely faithful in the most amazing ways! For one thing, He has shown me that He can provide for every financial need, regardless of what may come my way. I watched Him take care of thousands of doctors and hospital bills that I wasn't sure how we'd cover. Then, I have also seen Him offer and provide a peace that I couldn't have possibly comprehended through His Presence within my heart; that same Spirit that raised Jesus from the dead, *resurrection power within* me! That power has been there all along; I just didn't and hadn't accessed it in this manner before this point! That same Spirit and power resides within each one of us, of you, if you have received His forgiveness for your sins and have asked Him to come into your life. When He does, He comes with the greatest gift of all: the gift of Himself, His Spirit, His *resurrection power within* you! And the kicker to the whole thing is that He has promised that He will never leave you and will be with you, forever, with and through that same Spirit; again, that same *resurrection power* within you! What a promise!

Prayer for the Day: "Father, just as You led me to pray one time before, I offer up that same prayer today for me and for those who have and will read these words. Father, there is no way that we have the resources within us to try and navigate and deal with all of the stuff

THE HIP, THE HOSPITAL, AND THE HEALER

that this life throws at us each and every day. However, I thank You that You have already walked all of these roads that we still have to travel and have made a way for us to look to You, trust You, and depend upon Your *resurrection power within* each and every one of us who have the blessed privilege to know You! Thank You for promising that You'll never leave us and that You will, eventually, gather us all to Your home to be with You forever! We love You! In Jesus's name, amen!"

DAY 31 REFLECTION

"What Do You Want Me to Do for *You*?"

Focus: Personal Provision

"And seeing him, Jesus said, 'What do you want me to do for you?' And the blind man said to him, 'Rabboni, I want to regain my sight.' And Jesus said to him, 'Go, your faith has made you well.' Immediately, he regained his sight and *began* following Him on the road" (Mark 10:51–52, NASB).

"You lust and do not have, so you commit murder. You are envious and cannot obtain, so you fight and quarrel. You do not have because you do not ask" (James 4:2, NASB).

Ask, and it will be given to you; seek, and you will find; knock, and it will be opened to you. For ev-

THE HIP, THE HOSPITAL, AND THE HEALER

eryone who asks receives, and he who seeks, finds, and to him who knocks it will be opened. Or what man is there among you who, when his son asks for a loaf, will give him a stone? Or, if he asks for a fish, he will not give him a snake, will he? If you, then, being evil, know how to give good things to your children, how much more will your Father who is in heaven, give what is good to those who ask Him!

Matthew 7:7–11 (NASB)

Several years ago, I was sitting in a Missions Conference, listening to a young female missionary who was sharing her story of how the Lord had led her in her journey and how the particular ministry in which she was involved had come about. She told how she deeply desired to, one day, have a counseling center, a place where young ladies could come to find healing, wholeness, restoration, and peace within the country in which she and her husband served. On the particular day about which she spoke, she was sharing how she had been reading the account of the man known lovingly as *Blind Bartimaeus* and how the question that Jesus asked him in Mark 10:51 (NASB) was the same question that the Lord had, basically, pierced her heart with, as well, "What do you want Me to do for you?" Her response was to sit down with a sheet of paper and, literally, write down everything that she desired to see take place around her at that time; in fact, *exactly* what she wanted to see God do for *her*! What God was saying to her in that critical moment was, "I am the God of *personal provision*! I will *personally provide* for your *personal needs* with *personal provision!*"

In each of our lives, there will, most likely, come a point where we are faced with that same question, "What do you want Me to do for *you*?" I don't know about you, but the Father has been asking me that question a great deal lately. In fact, He continues to challenge me to be very specific about what it is that is in my heart and bring it to Him with detailed requests. None of us are exactly alike, so it isn't a stretch to say that we're each going to come to Him with many different wants, needs, hurts, and desires. Some of us today need healing for a specific physical malady. Some need a financial solution that, at this time, may appear hopeless. Others are looking for an answer to a family or relationship struggle for which there seems to be no apparent option to take. There are, likely, some who are reading these words and are simply looking for some emotional peace, a door of respite to get away from whatever it is that happens to be hounding their hearts, souls, and minds at this present time. That was the issue that faced the "thief on the cross," you know, the one who, during all that was happening, figured out that Jesus was, indeed, Who He said that He was and that He just might be able to redeem His heart and soul, even at that late hour. So, in Luke 23:42 (NIV), the thief prayed, "Jesus, remember me when You come into Your kingdom." In verse 23, Jesus responded with *personal provision*, "Truly I tell you, today you will be with me in paradise" (Luke 23:43, NIV).

Understand, there is nothing that is too big or too small, too large or too little, too much or too insignificant, too silly or too mundane about which to ask the Father. The question from the Lord Jesus still rings as true today as it did roughly two thousand years ago, "What do you want Me to do for you?" Regardless of how it looks to the outside world or to your own inside evaluator, "What do you want Him to do for you today?" (Yes, I keep on saying today because we're not promised tomorrow, and the reality is that if you need it, you don't need it tomorrow; you need it today!) So, ask the Lord and watch Him provide for you personally, with *personal provision*. Ask Him and watch to see what He does next and how He does it! It never hurts to ask. Just check with the "thief" (Luke 23:43). In fact, when you get to heaven, ask him yourself! He'll tell you it's true!

Prayer for the Day: "Father, I don't even begin to know how to process how much love there is that You have for me! I can't begin to understand just how You can love people who have, at times, ignorantly and at other times, willingly sinned against You and failed You again and again. However, I thank You that You have given us the record of Your Word to look to, lean on, and learn from so that You can reveal Yourself to us in demonstration of that supernatural love. Thank You that when You ask us, "What do you want Me to do for you?" You answer and respond with the kind of *personal provision* that only You can generate and produce. Yet, You do so with grace, mercy, and the kind of kindness that none of us deserve, ever! Today, please let me tell You how much I love You and appreciate everything that You do for me! I love You, Lord! In Jesus's precious name, amen!"

DAY 32 REFLECTION

"Taking Him at His Word!"

Focus: Trust His Word!

The royal official said, "Sir, come down before my child dies." "Go," Jesus replied, "your child will live." *The man took Jesus at His Word* and departed. While he was still on the way, his servants met him with the news that his boy was living. When he inquired as to the time when his son got better, they said to him, "Yesterday, at one in the afternoon, the fever left him." Then the father realized that this was the exact time at which Jesus had said to him, "Your son will live." So he and his whole household believed.

John 4:49–53 (NIV, author's italics)

"Every word is flawless; he is a shield to those who take refuge in him" (Proverbs 30:5, NIV).

We've all had those moments where we faced a difficult or a life-threatening situation for which there appears to be no real solution. Such was the case for the royal official in our passage whose son was, apparently, quite ill and for whom there seemed to be no one able to do anything to alter the imminent outcome. But then, he came to Jesus! With just a word, Jesus changed everything! Jesus told him simply, "Your child will live." 'Nuff said! No more words were needed, and nothing else to add! The simple reality of it all is that the man needed to do what we all need to do: take Him at His Word and *trust His Word!*

Now, I offer that simple solution because the Father has promised all throughout the Word of God that He is more than able and capable of taking care of and meeting any and every need that may come up in your life and in mine. For instance, as I write these words, I have a friend in the hospital who has had a tumor for a number of years that developed from a gunshot wound that he received during his time serving in our military in Vietnam. For several years, there have been repeated attempts to remove the tumor, but to no avail. However, not too long ago, he was led to believe that there was a great possibility that a particular surgeon truly might be able to remove the tumor safely and thus preserve my friend's life for a little while longer. As of yesterday, I received a text from his wife letting me know that the

THE HIP, THE HOSPITAL, AND THE HEALER

surgery had been a tremendous success and God had, indeed, blessed them with another answered prayer simply by *trusting in His Word!* So, think with me about some of the promises that are found in the Word of God that assure that we can *take Him at His word*. For instance:

Philippians 4:13 (NASB) tells us, "I can do all things through Him Who strengthens me."

Philippians 4:19 (NASB) says, "And my God will supply all your needs according to His riches in glory in Christ Jesus."

Genesis 18:14 (NASB) asks honestly, "Is anything too difficult for the LORD?"

Luke 1:37 (NASB) declares, "For nothing will be impossible with God."

In fact, Proverbs 30:5 (NASB) says, "Every word of God is pure. He is a shield to those who take refuge in him."

When my wife, Cindy, was growing up, her pastor, Ron Dunn, used to share that he would have conversations with people and hear them say, "God said it, I believe it, that settles it!" Then, Brother Dunn would amend their version of the story to say that the reality of the matter is that "God said it, and that settles it, whether I believe it or not!" Psalm 119:89 (NASB) says, "Forever, O LORD, your word is settled in heaven." The truth of the matter is that when the Lord God Himself speaks, what He says is done, final, complete, finished, over, accomplished, and coming to pass just as He said it would be! Today, whatever God says to you, trust Him! It will be just as He says it will be!

Prayer for the Day: "Father, we have so many different voices coming at us these days that, for many of us, we have lost the sense of which voice and whose word to trust in and believe. However, we thank You today that You are always trustworthy, never sidetracked, completely reliable, and will do exactly as You say that You will! We are so grateful that we have Your Word to read, memorize, claim, and rely on to be just as You said that it would be. Thank You that You never change and will take care of us, regardless of whatever comes our way. We desperately need You! We love You! In Jesus's name, amen!"

DAY 33 REFLECTION

"Be Still!"

Focus: Being Still!

"But Moses said to the people, 'Do not fear! Stand by and see the salvation of the LORD which He will accomplish for you today, for the Egyptians whom you have seen today, you will never see them again forever. The LORD will fight for you while you keep silent" (Exodus 14:13–14, NASB).

"You *need* not fight in this *battle*; station yourselves, stand and see the salvation of the LORD on your behalf, O Judah and Jerusalem. Do not fear or be dismayed; tomorrow go out to face them, for the LORD is with you" (2 Chronicles 20:17, NASB).

One of the stark realities of being in a hospital bed, in a wheelchair, on crutches, on a walker, on a cane, or any number of other transportation-assisted devices that we may be called upon to use when we can't walk freely, is the fact that for at least that period of time, we are going to need to get used to *being still* while we rehab, heal, or recuperate. The sheer fact of the matter is that you and I often think that we need to be, we *must be*, doing something for things to get done. Now, there's no question that while I was enduring the process of getting to the place where I could walk again, and I genuinely tried my best to do the part that I needed to do, I couldn't help but notice that there were things that I would, normally, have been doing, productive things, that I wasn't able to get done through that particular process. However, that didn't mean that I couldn't still be productive and fruitful, especially in the spiritual realm. While the Lord blessed me tremendously, He also reminded me that James 1:17 (NASB) says, "Every good and perfect thing given and every perfect gift is from above, coming down from the Father of lights, with whom there is no variation or shifting shadow." He also took me back to 1 Corinthians 4:7 (NASB), where the Apostle Paul admonished them, "For who regards you as superior? What do you have that you did not receive? And if you did receive it, why do you boast as if you had not received it?"

In each of the introductory scriptures above, there is a simple principle that we must not miss! God, our Precious Heavenly Father, gifts us with the strength and abilities that we have, and we do not do anything in and of our own! It is all from Him! So, even when we can do absolutely nothing to change, improve, or alter a situa-

THE HIP, THE HOSPITAL, AND THE HEALER

tion, He still can and will if we let Him! Sometimes, you and I need to just *be still* and let God be God!

Such was the case at the Red Sea with the Egyptian army. Moses and the children of Israel could do nothing to escape, fix, or improve their situation. Such was also the case for the Kingdom of Judah in 2 Chronicles 20. Yet, it is one of my favorite passages in the Word of God because it tells me two or three things that are critical to my walk with God. For one thing, there is not anything that God cannot handle, especially when we turn it over to Him and let Him do it, and do what He tells us to do: *be still!* The second thing is found in the words of the Lord Jesus, where He tells us in John 15:5 (NASB), "[A] part from Me, you can do nothing." The last time that I looked, nothing was pretty all-inclusive! In fact, Acts 17:28 (NASB) says, "[F]or in Him we live and move, and exist, as even some of your own poets have said. For we are also His children."

So, the next time that your hip goes out, or you have to have it replaced (and maybe two or three times, like me), stop for just a minute and remember that every movement that you have, every breath that you take, every sight that you see, everything that you are ever able to do in this life comes as a gift because He gave it to you. There comes a time when you and I need to just stop, *be still*, let God be God, and let God do what God does, which is everything for you and me! Yes, we are *so blessed!*

Prayer for the Day: "Father, for far too long, I have tried, albeit unsuccessfully, to live on my own, do things on my own, produce on my own, and make it on my own. As I have continually tried to do so, I have now come to a place where I realize that I can't do it; I am no longer physically able to even try to function without You. So, first of all, please forgive me for ever thinking that all of that was even possible. Then, thank You for bringing me to this place, a place where I am forced to *be still* and learn things about You that I would have never learned any other way! You have been so kind to me! You are so kind to me! Help me today to look to You, trust You, and let You be Who You are, the Lord of all creation! I love You! In Jesus's name, amen!"

DAY 34 REFLECTION

"Small Things!"

Focus: Little By Little!

"For who has despised the day of small things" (Zechariah 4:10a, NASB)?

"I will drive them out before you little by little until you become fruitful and take possession of the land" (Exodus 23:30, NASB).

Several years ago, I had the privilege of going to the country of Nepal after their earthquakes hit the country so destructively. While we were there, we sought to do everything that we could to serve the people and share the love of the Lord Jesus with them. However, with the religious climate there, there were certain things, such as sharing the gospel of the Lord Jesus openly, that we were encouraged not to do due to the threat of possible loss of life or, honestly, even potential decapitation. (Yeah, they are serious about their beliefs!) Because of the apparent threat of these outcomes, we were encouraged by those whom we served alongside to do acts of kindness, little things for people, all the while asking the Lord to open opportunities to share His love or to open the eyes of those that we sought to bless. Now, while it seemed at the time that we might not be accomplishing much, the reality was that with every simple touch and investment in their lives, at any level, He did indeed use those things to witness, bless, and communicate His love to them, even though we might not be able to see it, immediately. It was literally happening *little by little*, but it was making a difference!

In the book of Exodus, the Father told His children that He would give them the land, the victory "little by little," so that their land would not be desolate, nor would the beasts of the field be too numerous for them to overcome. In other words, He was giving them the victory, and He was also giving them the opportunity to get adjusted to the victory that He was giving them. Now, the reason that I even bring up these two particular illustrations is that when I had the original surgery, followed by the subsequent surgeries, there was this amazing peace in my heart that the Father was working and that He was going to walk me through this thing, regardless of how long it might take. As in so many things in life, as you and I are working our way through the challenges that come our way, the answers, solutions, and victories don't always come immediately. In fact, they are not always obvious, nor do they always sit right there on the surface to see. However, that doesn't mean that nothing is happening! The victories do come! In fact, while the progress seems, at times, quite slow, the reality is that He is working at all hours of the day and night, *little by little!*

Watch for the little steps, the tiny victories, the *small things, little by little!* You might be amazed at how God moves, works, and provides! Don't despise the small things!

Prayer for the Day: "Father, there are so many things that happen to us in this life for which there appears to be no apparent rationale. When those things do happen, I thank You that we are not left to our own devices or resources to try to figure out what You're doing or even why. Yet, we also realize that nothing happens that is random, accident, or happenstance. Being a Sovereign God, being 'The Sovereign God,' You are always working everything out according to Your plan! Thank You that You have promised that You have plans for each of us and that we are all part of that master plan! Today, please help us to continue to trust You through those unexplainable situations and know that nothing happens that You are not overseeing and ruling. You are working, even in the smallest details! What a great promise and great assurance! We love You! In Jesus's name, amen!"

DAY 35 REFLECTION

"No Fear of Bad News"

Focus: Unshaken!

Praise the LORD! How blessed is the man who fears the LORD, who greatly delights in His commandments. For he will never be shaken; the righteous will be remembered forever. He will not fear evil tidings; [NIV: They will have no fear of bad news.] His heart is steadfast, trusting in the LORD.

Psalm 112:1, 6–7 (NASB)

"My soul *waits* in silence for God only; from Him is my salvation. He only is my rock and my salvation, my stronghold; I shall not be greatly shaken" (Psalm 62:1–2, NASB).

Being a pastor, I have told people often that I have the greatest occupation in the world! I truly mean that!

THE HIP, THE HOSPITAL, AND THE HEALER

Oh, that doesn't mean that it is always easy, or rosy, or smooth sailing, as they say. However, I absolutely love doing what I do, as it has provided me with a lifetime of amazing joy, seeking to help people on a daily basis, with no two days being exactly alike! One of the most incredible things has been the privilege and opportunity to watch people's understanding and perspective change as they wrap their heads and hearts around the love of God and His provision and sovereignty in their lives, realizing that He will *always* come through, regardless of the need!

I have also shared with my church family that when my telephone rings anytime between the hours of 11:00 p.m. at night and 5:00 a.m. in the morning, it is *rarely* good news, as usually, something bad has happened, or someone has passed away. So, I have learned to not panic when that kind of phone call comes, understanding that God, the Father, has promised that He will bless and take care of us, no matter what the news is! Not too long ago, we were sitting in a grief recovery meeting, and I read the verses from Psalm 62 to the people gathered there. One of the sweet ladies sitting there in the meeting stopped me in my tracks and said to me, "Read that again! Where is that found in Scripture?" So, I repeated the passage for her and emphasized the fact that the Lord promised through His psalmist that, no matter what comes my way, "I shall not be greatly shaken."

Now, that doesn't mean that bad, tough, or difficult times don't come, as we all know that they do! However, what it does mean is what He has already shown to me and proven to me over and over through countless struggles and hard times: "Because He is with me, I have *no fear of bad news*, nor do I need to fear because *I will never be shaken!*" What an amazing promise to wrap our trust in: "You and I are covered. *We don't ever have to be shaken!*"

Prayer for the Day: "Father, I am so grateful to You that there will never come into our lives a situation that You are not in control of, totally! Since Your Word tells us that nothing is too hard for You, then we can truly rest and relax in the fact that You are completely dependable and capable of handling any and everything that happens to us, as nothing just randomly 'happens' to come there. You either ordain or allow all that we might encounter in this life. So, we know that we are completely in Your hands, regardless of what we run into on a daily basis. Thank You so much that You are watching over us in every situation, no matter how it looks. You are here! You are God! You are sovereign! You are in control! You are more than capable! We are completely covered and cared for! We love You! In Jesus's name, amen!"

DAY 36 REFLECTION

"He Was Just Like Us!"

Focus: Just Like Us!

Therefore, since we have a great high priest who has passed through the heavens, Jesus the Son of God, let's hold firmly to our confession. For we do not have a high priest who cannot sympathize with our weaknesses, but One who has been tempted in all things just as we are, yet without sin. Therefore, let's approach the throne of grace with confidence, so that we may receive mercy and find grace for help at the time of our need.

Hebrews 4:14–16 (NASB)

"In the days of His humanity, He offered up both prayers and pleas with loud crying and tears to the One able to save Him from death, and He was heard because of His devout behavior" (Hebrews 5:7, NASB).

"See My hands and My feet, that it is I Myself: touch Me and see, because a spirit does not have flesh and bones as you *plainly* see that I have" (Luke 24:39, NASB).

For the longest time, I have been personally touched by the fact that I identify with people who have experienced the same things that I experienced. For instance, we have traveled the same roads, walked the same paths, had the same struggles, experienced the same temptations, fought the same battles, cried the same tears, and experienced the same life struggles so that we can truly understand what each other is going through. We identify with one another! When I read the stories of the Lord Jesus, it absolutely blesses my life because I find in him the One who really understands what's happening in my heart at any given moment! I see Him cry at the loss of a close friend. I see Him living the kind of life that others are, hopefully, drawn to, and I want to try to do the same thing. I see Him making a difference, an eternal difference in the lives of those around Him, and I desire to do just like He did!

After His resurrection, if you'll recall with me, Thomas wasn't with the rest of the disciples when they saw Jesus for the first time. So, when Thomas heard about Jesus's appearance, he didn't believe it initially but wanted to have his own visual reinforcement to verify for himself that Jesus was truly alive! Just a short time later, the disciples had all gathered again, and on this occasion, Jesus, once again, appeared! Jesus made His direct appeal to Thomas to see Him, touch Him, grasp Him, and know for certain that it was indeed Jesus Himself! When it was all said and done, not only was Thomas convinced, but he realized that Jesus truly was resurrected from the dead, that the human body had come to life! He really was human, *just like us!*

Now, while we readily acknowledge that Jesus is indeed both God and man, we highlight the fact here that He was fully man to acknowledge the truth that He actually was *just like us* in the sense that, as Philippians 2:8 (NASB) tells us, He "emptied Himself, taking upon Himself the form of a bondservant, and being made in the likeness of men." When you and I go through the trials of life, regardless of what they are, we can take tremendous comfort in the fact that we have Someone Who truly understands, identifies, and walks through each and every one of those situations because He came down to us and walked through this same life that we are going through, *just like us!*

(*Disclaimer*: On one hand, I readily acknowledge that He is *nothing like us* because, after all, we are talking about God Almighty! However, on the other hand, I think that it is most critical that we fully understand that He fully understands and identifies with everything that you and I are experiencing, as He has already been here and done all of this! In that vein, and in the most genuine sense of the word, He truly is *just like us!*)

Prayer for the Day: "Father, I thank You that You sent Your only Son to pay a price and make a way for me so that I could know You personally. Jesus, I can't begin to thank You enough for everything that You went through: as a newborn baby, as a small child, as a young adult, as one *just like us*, and as both the Son of God and the Savior of the world, to offer Your forgiveness and Your free gift of eternal life to me and to those who trust You! I can't begin to fathom or imagine what all that really cost You! Please forgive me when I take it for granted, or when I'm presumptuous, or when I'm unappreciative or apathetic. I know I don't deserve Your love, nor do I deserve the sacrifice You made or the price You paid! But thank You again for what You did for me! I love You! I worship You! In Jesus's name, amen!"

DAY 37 REFLECTION

"Lessons from a Thorn!"

Focus: Irritating Teacher!

"Because of the surpassing greatness of the revelations, for this reason, to keep me from exalting myself, there was given me a thorn in the flesh, a messenger of Satan to torment me—to keep me from exalting myself" (2 Corinthians 12:7, NASB).

"Pray without ceasing" (1 Thessalonians 5:17, NASB).

You ever have one of those splinters in your hand; you know, the pesky kind that slides straight in under your fingernail and, regardless of what you go in there after it with, you just can't get it out? Yeah, me too! Another name for those kinds of aggravating visitors to your system is *thorn*, which I have heard described as "a source of continual irritation or suffering." Yes, sir, we've all had them. The Apostle Paul had one, too. Now,

I've been asked numerous times, "What do you think that Paul's *thorn* was?" I have absolutely no idea! The reality is that I truly believe that the Father purposely didn't tell us what Paul's *thorn* was so that, regardless of what our particular *thorn* might happen to be on any given day, Paul's example, admonitions, and instructions would pertain to and apply to each one of us in our own *thorn*.

At times, that's kind of how I felt about that hip condition that I had developed: a *thorn*, a sticker in my side! Yet, I came to realize that this little aggravation that I had going on on the side of my body, this life-threatening irritant, was being used by the Father as just that, an *irritating teacher*! It reminded me of the truth found in Hebrews 5:8 (NASB) concerning the Lord Jesus, Himself, when that verse declares quite clearly to us, "Although He was a Son, He learned obedience from the things which He suffered." That *thorn*, those *thorns* that come into our lives, serve as *irritating teachers* to teach us about things that we would have never learned otherwise. It can impart to us some vivid lessons if we'll let it. In fact, think of it with me in this way:

A *thorn* can "*puncture pride*" [2 Corinthians 12:7 (NASB) says, "to keep me from exalting myself"].

A *thorn* can "*prompt prayer*" [2 Corinthians 12:8 (NASB) says, "I implored the Lord three times that it might leave me"].

A *thorn* can *"prepare peace"* [2 Corinthians 12:9 (NASB) says, "My grace is sufficient for you"]. A thorn can prepare the way in a believer's heart to call on the Lord. As Philippians 4 tells us, when and as we pray, God promises His peace as His response and our desired outcome!

A *thorn* can *"promote praise"* [2 Corinthians 12:9 (NASB) says, "Most gladly therefore I will rather boast about my weaknesses"].

And a *thorn* can *"produce perspective"* [2 Corinthians 12:10 (NASB) says, "for when I am weak, then I am strong"].

Today, I have no idea what kind of *thorn* has entered your life. However, don't lose sight of the fact that, if it's there, the Father has either chosen it, ordained it, or allowed it. Regardless, He's in charge of even the smallest splinter of a *thorn* that comes into our lives, and He's likely using it to teach us something either about us or Himself that we can probably never learn any other way! Thank You today, Lord, that there is a lesson in every *thorn*!

Prayer for the Day: "Lord God, I can't even begin to fathom all of the ways that You seek to work in our lives as You remind us that Your thoughts are not our thoughts, nor are Your ways our ways! We see in Your choices and activities a creativity that we could never understand or match, regardless of how hard we try! You see things so much more deeply and in a much more far-reaching way than we can ever truly comprehend. So, we are thankful that we don't have to figure it all out! All You ask us to do is to trust and obey! Please help us all to do that today to bring glory to Your name! Thank You for each and every *thorn* that teaches us something brand new about You! We love You! We need You today and every day of our lives! In Jesus's name, amen!"

DAY 38 REFLECTION

"The Good Old Days!"

Focus: But Then I Recall!

"I think of the good old days, long since ended, when my nights were filled with joyful songs. I search my soul and ponder the difference now" (Psalm 77:5–6, NLT).

"And I said, 'This is my fate; the Most High has turned his hand against me.' But then I recall all you have done, O LORD. I remember your wonderful deeds of long ago" (Psalm 77:10–11, NLT).

One of the key lessons that is learned in a time of difficulty is the fact that you and I need never try to establish or determine our belief system or deduce our theology from the center of, or from the middle of, a time of difficulty. For one thing, most of the time, when something in our lives has "gone in the tank," so to speak, we rarely have all of the information that we need to adequately or accurately interpret the exact nature of whatever is happening to us right then. Oh, we may have a basic idea of what is happening, or we may be given a glimpse of whatever it is that we are dealing with. But we rarely have enough information to try to make an accurate depiction or understanding of the events going on at the time. The reason that this principle becomes so important is the fact that, often, we find ourselves trying to interpret stuff that we're seeing, and we can't see all that God can see. So, consequently, we often end up misevaluating some critical points and facts and totally misunderstanding exactly what's going on. Then, we begin to think about those times that we think were better, what the psalmist calls "the good old days." Now, you remember times like those that are described here: "when my nights were filled with joyful song" (Psalm 77:6, NLT). We can all think of times that we thought were better, more desirable, or absolutely perfect! Then, we compare that to whatever is happening to us at that particular moment, and we moan, gripe, lament, and wish that we could either go back there or experience something different from whatever is happening right then!

When this happens, we're oftentimes pretty sure that God has either dissed us or done us wrong in one way or another. *But then I recall* all You have done, O Lord! I begin to remember just what blessings I have experienced, what answered prayers I have witnessed, what provisions I have seen, what acts of kindness I have been given from the precious hand of the Lord, and I remember Your wonderful deeds of long ago. Henry Blackaby calls them "spiritual markers" from the Lord, those visible, tangible indicators that His hand has provided whatever you and I may have needed at the time! There is rarely a day that goes by that I couldn't find something that is less than what I wished that it would be. In fact, each time that I had to go to the "infectious disease doctor's office" every day to kill the infection that had so deeply invaded my hip, I had that exact kind of feeling going in there. *But then I recalled* the blessings that God had given to me and the difficulties that others had that they were dealing with. *Yes, I recalled* the goodness of the Lord, and each time, I was uplifted, encouraged, and inspired because I realized that He is truly in charge of everything in my life and has promised His immeasurable blessings on me and in everything having to do with me because He said that it would be so! What an incredible blessing! Don't just believe that He only worked in "the good old days"! He's still working just as clearly and just as promised today! What has He done for you in the past?

Prayer for the Day: "Father, sometimes I get lost in the days gone by because I truly do remember just how blessed I have been, and it seems that those were better days than these that I'm seeking to walk through right now. However, I realize that You haven't changed one bit and that You're still the same, regardless of how things might look to the rest of the world. So, please help me and help us to see with a fresh set of our own eyes just how much "in the present" You are functioning today! It may seem at first that You are no longer working like You were. *But then I recall* Your mercy and Your goodness, and I know that You are, truly, still the same! Please help us and bless us today! We desperately need You! We love You, Lord! In Jesus's name, amen!"

DAY 39 REFLECTION

"Just the Right Word!"

Focus: With a Word!

"Like apples of gold in settings of silver is a word spoken in right circumstances" (Proverbs 25:11, NASB).

"The LORD God has given me the tongue of disciples, that I may know how to sustain the weary one *with a word*. He awakens Me morning by morning. He awakens My ear to listen as a disciple" (Isaiah 50:4, NASB, italics added).

"Let your speech always be with grace, as though seasoned with salt, so that you will know how you should respond to each person" (Colossians 4:6, NASB).

In Matthew 8, there is the story of a centurion, a man who was a leader in a Roman army who commanded a military squad of somewhere around eighty to a hundred soldiers, also called Roman legionnaires. In the account found in Matthew 8, the centurion, the commander, comes to Jesus to plead for the healing of one of his men, a servant of his who had, obviously, become quite ill. So, he comes to Jesus to ask for Jesus's help. However, he does so in an unusual manner. He doesn't ask Jesus to come to where the man is lying ill. He says to Jesus in verse 8, "Lord, I am not worthy for You to come under my roof, but just say the word and my servant will be healed" (Matthew 8:8, NASB). While we don't pretend to be Jesus, He has told us that He has given all authority to you and me, and when we speak, and especially when we seek Him and speak with and in His power, He is quite often speaking right through us, and it is amazing what can be done *with a word!*

When you are in a hospital or medical setting, there is nothing that is better for the heart, mind, will, and emotions, whether it is for you, as the patient, or someone close to you, than to hear that you are healing, getting better, getting well, and getting close to going home! It is just the right word! When you are in a difficult spot in life, there is often nothing that goes further and does more good than for someone to give you just that piece of encouragement that you need *with a word!* In fact, there are times when someone encourages us with *just that word,* and that is the very thing that we need to hear! Sometimes, that word that is spoken to us will come to us in the form of a question, such as, "How are you doing?" or "Are you all right?" or "What can I do to help you?" Often, those could be some of the sweetest words that can ever be uttered by human lips!

Other times, the word that is offered may be in the form of a word of encouragement, such as, "You've got this!" or "God's got this!" It could be framed, as we've alluded to earlier, as the motivation that is offered by Nemo's friend Dory in the little children's movie *Finding Nemo* as she tells him when all looks totally hopeless, "Just keep swimming, just keep swimming, just keep swimming!" It is so reminiscent of the truth found in Ecclesiastes 4:9–12, where he says,

> Two are better than one because they have a good return for their labor. For if either of them fails, the one will lift up his companion. But woe to the one who falls when there is not another to lift him up. Furthermore, if two lie down together they keep warm but how can one be warm *alone*? And if one can overpower him who is alone, two can resist him. A cord of three *strands* is not quickly torn apart.
>
> Ecclesiastes 4:9–12 (NASB)

It's pretty amazing what one person can do *with a word*! Just one word, spoken at precisely the right time, in the right way, for the right reason, to the right person can completely alter the course of that life! While only God can actually orchestrate that, He has given to you and me what 2 Corinthians 5:18 (NASB) calls "the ministry of reconciliation." And it all begins with and is empowered *with a word*! Don't ever sell yourself short regarding how the Lord might choose to use you to share a word with someone in just the right setting! You never know; you might just be the one to reset the pattern of a life for the Lord and His purposes *with a word*!

Prayer for the Day: "Father, we read in Your Word about how often You spoke the Word to someone and totally overhauled their heart and life! Today, we come to You and confess that we are *all* in need today of just that Word that only You can speak that will make an eternal difference. Please allow us through Your Word and through Your Precious Holy Spirit to hear that Word that will alter the course of the eternity of all of us! You've proven over and over what You can do *with a word*! Please do it again today! We love You! In Jesus's name, amen!"

DAY 40 REFLECTION

"Safely Home!"

Focus: Healed and Delivered!

"The Lord will rescue me from every evil deed, and will bring me safely to His heavenly kingdom; to Him be the glory for ever and ever" (2 Timothy 4:18, NASB).

Just a few days ago, I was assisting a family in a memorial service for a gentleman who had been working at a factory. He was awakened at 3:30 a.m. every morning by an alarm that alerted him to the fact that he needed to go ahead and get up and get around to be on time to get to work at around 5:00 a.m. The reason that I even bring this up is that his wife took the opportunity to speak at his memorial. She shared the fact that not only did he wake up at 3:30 a.m. each morning, but so did she since she slept right next to him every night! With a broken heart and tear-stained eyes, she shared how they would both awaken each morning when the alarm went off. He would go ahead and get up and make his way to his work. Then, when he arrived, he would immediately call his wife to let her know that he had, once again, arrived at his job safely!

The thing that grabbed my attention was her declaration that on that same morning, the morning that we were meeting to have his memorial service, his alarm had gone off, as it normally did. However, the difference in this particular morning was that she remained awake for quite some time, yet his call, obviously, never came! The interesting part of her story and the implication was that it left her with at least a little bit of wonder as to "if" and "whether" he had arrived safely, *anywhere!* In the course of the service, it became quite apparent that this guy had a true relationship with the Lord Jesus and that he was a regular at a Bible-teaching church, which he truly enjoyed and was looking forward to the day when he would leave this life and go to be with the Lord! So, as I sat there and took in all that was being said and inferred about his death and departure, I asked his wife if she would allow me to say something to her based on what she had already communicated to us. She told me that, "Yes," that was fine! So, I said, "Remember what you said about him arriving every day safely?" She nodded in the affirmative. So, I told her, "Please allow me to assure you that, based on the Person, nature, character, and promises of Almighty God, Who never lies [Numbers 23:19, Titus 1:2; Hebrews 6:18], *your precious husband has arrived home safely!*" Then, I quoted for her 2 Timothy 4:18 (NASB), "The Lord will rescue me from every deed, and will bring me safely to His heavenly kingdom: to Him be the glory for ever and ever." Even through her deep and obvious pain, she managed to form a small smile and mouthed to me, "Thank you!" I reminded her that I realized that nothing fixed the fact that he was no longer with her and us. Yet, I also asked her to allow me to encourage her not to overlook the promises of God! He, alone, could and can bring the comfort, peace, and assurance that she was looking for and that you and I are looking for! He can and will get us *safely home!* Her husband was and is ultimately *healed and delivered*, and the fact of the matter was and is that she will get to be with him again very soon!

As I pondered everything that I had seen, I also couldn't help but look at the situation in my own life, and with this hip thing that had brought me so much insight and understanding, I think, "I, too, am now totally *healed and delivered!*" How blessed can you be? Well, I'm totally blessed! Thank You, Almighty God and Father! As His Word says, "To Him be the glory both now and to the day of eternity" (2 Peter 3:18, NASB). Amen!

Prayer for the Day: "Father, through all of this time that You and I have been sharing regarding this hip and the lessons and reflections that it has provided, I have been reminded again and again of how much You love me and how 'deeply' Your love runs in both my life and in this world. I have prayed for the people reading these words so that they might glean the lessons and insights that You want them to learn, hopefully, many of the same things that You have so graciously shown me! I thank You that Your Word tells us that 'there is no partiality with God' (Romans 2:11, NASB), a.k.a. that You are "no respecter of persons." Lord, I worship You! Just as You have over and over safely taken Your loved ones home to be with You in Your kingdom and Your heaven, You have promised that You will do exactly the same thing for me and my brothers and sisters who remain here on the earth until the Lord Jesus returns! Father, please use these lessons and insights to be an encouragement to those who read! We desperately need You to help us navigate through the remaining waters that we call life! We look to You for everything! I thank You that I am now, presently, *healed and delivered*! Thank You that You will lead us, direct us, bless us, and get us *safely home*! In Jesus's mighty name, amen!"

"In the Event of..."

So, let's suppose that you've read these words, but you have never actually been what Jesus calls in the Bible "born again."

"Jesus replied, 'Very truly I tell you, no one can see the kingdom of God unless they are born again'" (John 3:3, NIV). You'd like to receive Him into your life but are unsure as to just how to do so. To receive Jesus into your heart and life, please understand these things:

1. God truly loves you so much, and if you are feeling any urge or inkling toward Him, it's because He is reaching out to you!

"No one can come to me unless the Father who sent me draws them, and I will raise them up at the last day" (John 6:44, NIV). The Father is drawing you to Himself!

2. We have all sinned and have fallen short of God's righteous ideal for our lives.

"For all have sinned and fall short of the glory of God" (Romans 3:23, NIV). Also, the "wages" or "pay" or "outcome" of our sins is "death, spiritual death," being separated from the Presence and love of God in hell, forever!

"For the wages of sin is death, but the gift of God is eternal life in Christ Jesus our Lord" (Romans 6:23, NIV).

3. Jesus died on the cross to pay the penalty for the sins that you and I have or will ever commit!

"For God so loved the world that he gave his one and only Son, that whoever believes in him shall not perish but have eternal life" (John 3:16, NIV).

"God made him who had no sin to be sin for us, so that in him we might become the righteousness of God" (2 Corinthians 5:21, NIV).

4. We must individually "acknowledge" our sin, "believe" in the sacrifice that He made for us in our behalf, and "receive" His gift of forgiveness and eternal life that He offers to us by calling out to Him in prayer or confession of our sin, submitting to His Lordship, and receiving of His life and gift of eternal life into our own hearts and lives!

5. If you are unsure as to how to pray to do so, please read and pray the following prayer. This

prayer, or prayer in general, is not magic, but its information is your own way of communicating to the Lord that you want Him to please forgive your sins and come into your life with His gift of salvation! So, please follow this prayer and talk to the Lord by praying it!

Pray the Following:

"Lord God, I thank You that You love me. Thank You for sending Jesus to die on the cross to save me from my sins. I confess to You that I have sinned, and I ask You to forgive me for my sin. I repent of my sins (I turn away from them, and I turn toward You), and I thank You for forgiving me! Jesus, would You please come into my heart to be my Savior and Lord? Thank You for saving me, and thank You for coming into my life! Just like You promised in the Bible, always let me know that You're there! Thank You for the promise of eternal life and that You've promised You'll never leave me! In Jesus's name, amen!"

If you prayed to receive Him, or for questions, comments, communication, or contacts for speaking engagements, please email me at lgdelay@cox.net!

Thank you!

—Dr. Larry G. DeLay

Dr. Larry G. DeLay:
Educational Background

Universities/Seminaries:

Southeastern State University
Durant, Oklahoma
Fall 1973 – Spring 1974

Oklahoma Baptist University
Shawnee, Oklahoma
Fall 1974 - Spring 1978
B.A. in Religion
"Cum Laude"

The University of Tulsa
Tulsa, Oklahoma
Fall 1983

Northeastern State University
Tahlequah, Oklahoma
Fall 1982 - Spring 1983
Spring 1984 - Fall 1984
B.A. in Music - Vocal Performance
"Cum Laude"

Trinity Theological Seminary
Newburgh, Indiana
Master of Divinity
"Summa cum Laude"

Doctor of Ministry - Expository Preaching - 1991
"Summa cum Laude" - (Stephen Olford - Instructor)

Master's International School of Divinity
Newburgh, Indiana
Doctor of Biblical Studies – Biblical Counseling - 2009
"Magna cum Laude"

New Orleans Baptist Theological Seminary
New Orleans, Louisiana
Spring 2010

DR. LARRY G. DeLAY

Midwestern Baptist Theological Seminary,
Kansas City, Missouri
Fall 2010

Louisiana Baptist University and Theological Seminary
Doctor of Philosophy in Theology
Graduation Date: May 2025

Bibliography

Blackaby, Henry. *Experiencing God*. Tennessee: B&H Publishing Group, 2008

Printed in the USA
CPSIA information can be obtained
at www.ICGtesting.com
LVHW010802080524
779241LV00010B/535